M000247641

365 Tales From ISLAM

Ziya Us Salam

Om
KIDZ

An imprint of Om Books International

First published in 2019 by

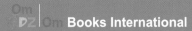 **Books International**

Corporate & Editorial Office
A-12, Sector 64, Noida 201 301
Uttar Pradesh, India
Phone: +91 120 477 4100
Email: editorial@ombooks.com
Website: www.ombooksinternational.com

Sales Office
107, Ansari Road, Darya Ganj
New Delhi 110 002, India
Phone: +91 11 4000 9000
Email: sales@ombooks.com
Website: www.ombooks.com

© Om Books International 2019

ALL RIGHTS RESERVED. No part of this book may be reproduced or
transmitted in any form by any means, electronic or mechanical, including
photocopying and recording, or by any information storage and retrieval
system, except as may be expressly permitted in writing by the publisher.

Disclaimer: **The visuals used in this book attempt to evoke the spirit of
Islam. They bear no resemblance to any of the prophets of Islam, their
wives, companions or the four caliphs.**

ISBN: 9789352764051

Printed in India

10 9 8 7 6 5 4 3 2 1

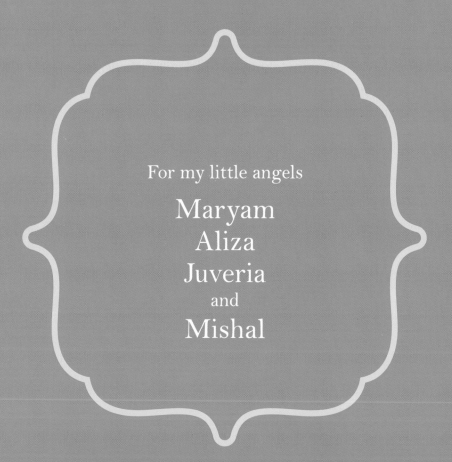

For my little angels

Maryam
Aliza
Juveria
and
Mishal

Assalam-u-alaikum!

Islam means peace; the basic greeting in Islam is a salutation of peace. This peace though comes not just from being healthy and happy, but with complete surrender to the will of Allah. That is what Islam means. The Quran provides the bedrock of the faith. Revealed to Prophet Muhammad, the Quran is for the entire humanity, not just Muslims. The Muslims have no monopoly over it.

Said to be among the youngest of faiths, Islam is actually the oldest. The first man to step on earth, Adam is regarded by the faithful as the first prophet. After Allah sent Adam, He did not leave mankind unattended. Over a period of time, prophets and messengers were sent to all people across the world. The prophets and messengers were separated by thousands of miles and years, but followed the same religion and gave the same teaching: Worship one god, that is, Allah and do not associate any partners with Him. All of them faced hardship, adversity and even cruelty. All of them turned to Allah for help, believing that Allah's help is sufficient. Finally, Allah sent Prophet Muhammad with whom the line of prophets and messengers was completed. The Prophet communicated Allah's true guidance afresh. Some people followed him, others did not. Many of his followers were killed, some migrated. The Prophet himself, with a bunch of companions, performed Hijrat, and went to Madinah. Yet, he never equivocated, never swerved from the path chosen for mankind.

This book '365 Tales from Islam' is a small attempt to recount the stories of some of the prophets of Islam, their teachings, the life and times of Prophet Muhammad (PBUH), his battles, his values, and the guidance he provided.

I have consulted Hadiths from Bukhari Sharif, Sahi Muslim, Daud, Tirmidhi and Ibn Maajah. The Quran with its tafsir by Mufti Abdul Dayam and Abul Ala Mawdudi's Towards Understanding Islam were frequently consulted for many stories about the prophets, as were translations of the Quran by Maulana Wahiduddin Khan and Prof Syed Vickar Ahmed.

One little request to all children who read this book, or who get it read to them: always say 'Peace be Upon Him' at the mention of the Prophet's name. Similarly, say 'May Allah be Pleased with Him/Her' after the names the companions of Prophet Muhammad (PBUH) or his wives. For other prophets, we should say, Peace/Blessings on You.

Happy reading!

Contents

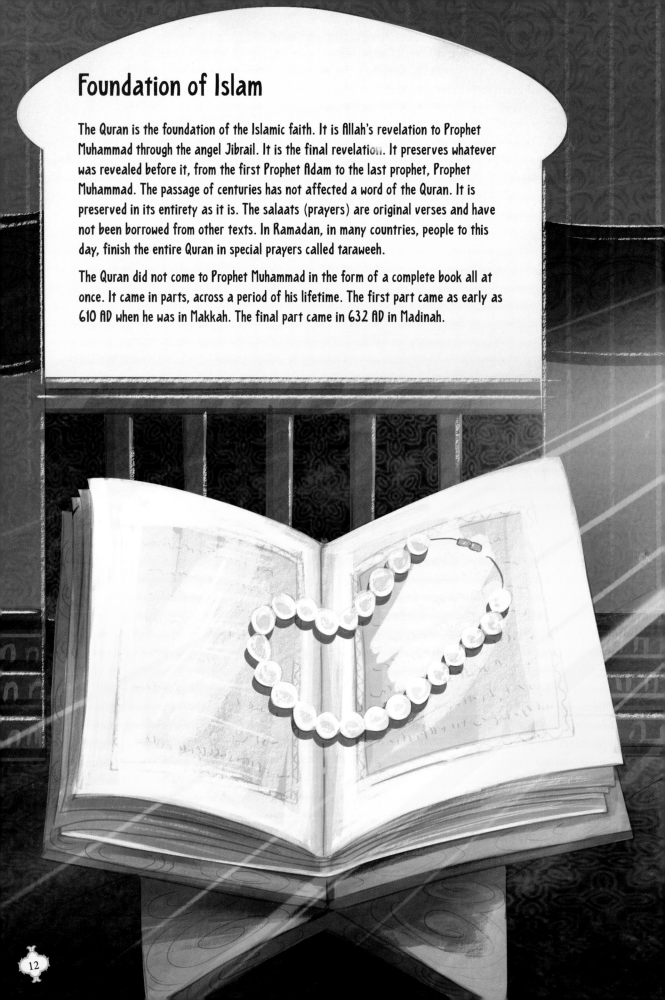

Foundation of Islam

The Quran is the foundation of the Islamic faith. It is Allah's revelation to Prophet Muhammad through the angel Jibrail. It is the final revelation. It preserves whatever was revealed before it, from the first Prophet Adam to the last prophet, Prophet Muhammad. The passage of centuries has not affected a word of the Quran. It is preserved in its entirety as it is. The salaats (prayers) are original verses and have not been borrowed from other texts. In Ramadan, in many countries, people to this day, finish the entire Quran in special prayers called taraweeh.

The Quran did not come to Prophet Muhammad in the form of a complete book all at once. It came in parts, across a period of his lifetime. The first part came as early as 610 AD when he was in Makkah. The final part came in 632 AD in Madinah.

Though addressed to the entire humanity, the Quran was revealed in Arabic. Hence, it is only the Arabic original that has the beauty and symphony of the recitation of the book. The Quran that we possess today is exactly the Quran edition prepared on the orders of Caliph Abu Bakr. Caliph Usman sent several copies of the Quran to other empires and cities. When the Quran was revealed, it was written down in Arabic qirtas. At the same time, some people started memorising it. With that started the tradition of being a hafiz — one who has memorised the Quran and all its 114 chapters and over 6,000 verses. Yet it is a book that is to be read slowly. One has to understand its words and explore their meaning, their interpretation. The Quran itself says, 'Recite the Quran slowly and distinctly.'

The Revelation

At the end of a long day, Prophet Muhammad would go to a cave called Hira. In the cave, he would think about the purpose of human life. He wondered about questions like why humans were created, and where everybody would go after living on earth. As he would sit there in absolute peace and quiet, he would contemplate in deep thought. One night, Angel Jibrail visited him. The angel uttered, 'Iqra bismi rabbilkallazi khalaq (Read in the name of your Lord who created).' The Prophet was mortified as he could not read or write. But Jibrail insisted that he must read. So he began to repeat the words that came to him with the angel's help. Thus came about the first verses of the Quran.

Jibrail went away soon after.

The event was so overwhelming that it left the Prophet shivering from head to foot.Still sweating, he came down to his wife Khadijah who, though afraid, stood by him like a rock. She covered him with a blanket, assuring him that Allah had a purpose for him as he was a man of integrity and had been helpful to others. The Quran was revealed across 23 years with the Prophet breathing his last soon after the revelation of the last verses.

The First Man on Earth

Allah created this beautiful earth with all its plants and animals. He created mountains, valleys and desert lands. When He needed to create something, he would say, 'Be,' and it became. Then, Allah decided to create something special. This time He created the human form with His own hands and in His own image. He called him Adam. He made Adam unique in comparison to His other creations and gave him the fountain of knowledge that even the angels did not have. All angels bowed to Adam as commanded by Allah, except Iblis, also known as Satan. The fountain of knowledge would sprout wisdom bestowed upon those who could use that knowledge in a loving, compassionate manner. Thus, Allah's favourite being, Adam, came to be created.

Miracles and Magic

Allah sent Musa, popularly called Moses, to the kingdom of Firaun to spread the message of light and truth. Firaun was a powerful king. He tolerated no criticism, and insisted that all the subjects bow to him. When Allah asked Musa to go to his court, Musa asked for help. He wanted to take his brother Haroon with him, as his speech was not so clear. His request was granted by Allah who also taught him a few tricks better than any magician or sorcerer in Firaun's land. So Musa was sent to spread the message of Allah in the land where everybody was expected to worship the king. In kingship lay godliness for Firaun. It was to change soon with the arrival of Musa.

Paradise Lost

When Allah asked the angels to bow to Adam, they all did. Except Iblis, often called Satan or Shaitan. Iblis refused, arguing with Allah, 'You made me with fire. Man is made from clay. Why should I bow to him?'

Then Allah asked Adam to go and dwell in Paradise. He ended Adam's desolation there by creating the first woman, Hawwa. Thus came about the first man and the first woman as husband and wife. They were allowed to eat of all that they pleased but stay away from a tree. One day, Iblis tempted Adam and his wife to try a fruit from the forbidden tree. Adam realised his mistake and sought Allah's pardon. They were pardoned and sent to the earth where Adam, his wife and his progeny were to dwell for a limited time and return to Allah.

Thus the first man set foot in the world. And pray, where did he first come? Sri Lanka. The first man in the world, the first prophet of Islam set foot in Sri Lanka, as is widely believed.

The Burial Tradition

Muslims across the world bury their dead. There is no casket, just a shroud which is wrapped around the body. This tradition of laying to rest started with the first man on earth, Adam. It is said that when the angels of death came to take the soul of Adam, his wife clung to him before he asked her to move away. The angels then took out the soul of Adam, washed his body, put on a shroud and embalmed him. Then they dug a grave. The angels said a prayer before putting Adam in the grave, and filled it with clay.

Before leaving, they said, 'O children of Adam! This will be your tradition (of burial/last rites).' The tradition has not changed since then.

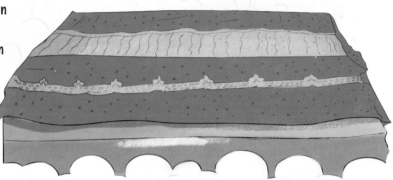

Cain and Abel

Initially, Adam had two sons, Cain and Abel. The Quran relates their story in these words, 'And recite to them the true story of the two sons of Adam, when they each offered a sacrifice, and it was accepted from one of them and not accepted from the other. The latter said, 'I will kill you.' The former retorted, 'Allah accepts only from those who are pious.' And he promised not to raise his hand at his brother even if the latter were to kill him. Cain then killed Abel. He, however, did not know how to hide the body of his brother. Allah sent a raven to show him how to scratch the earth to bury the body. Seeing this, Cain became regretful. He wondered how come a raven knew more than him.

Why was the offering of one brother accepted, and not of the other? It was a simple fruit of intended actions. Abel was a shepherd and he offered a fat lamb. Cain offered a bundle of the worst crop. Their intentions mattered.

Sheeth Continues Adam's Work

Sheeth was the third son of Adam. When Adam was about to die, he made a covenant with Sheeth; also called Shith, the Gift of Allah. Adam taught Sheeth the ways of worship and about the hours of day and night. He taught him about a flood which was about to come. The angels consoled Sheeth at the death of Adam.

Sheeth was Allah's Prophet too. Fifty scriptures were sent down to him. He carried on Adam's work, before assigning the task to his son Anoosh as he prepared to leave the world. Incidentally, legend has it that the entire mankind hails from Sheeth, as he was the only son of Adam to be blessed with progeny. His existence was said to be a consolation for the death of Abel who was killed by Cain.

Lineage of Mankind

Adam and his sons lived a really long life. Adam himself is said to have lived for 930 years. He was 130 years old when his third son Sheeth, was born. Sheeth was 165 years old when he was blessed with a son called Enos. He lived for more than 800 years after Anoosh was born!

Anoosh too had a son, Kenan, when he was aged 90. He lived on for another 815 years. In comparison, Kenan was blessed with a son early. He was 70 years old when his son Mahalalel was born. Mahalalel had a son called Jared when he was 65. Incidentally, Mahalalel is said to have built the city of Babylon.

Jared was around 162 years when his son Enoch, otherwise called Idris, was born. Methusaleh was born to Idris when the latter was 65. Methusaleh himself was 187 when his son Lamech was born. Lamech son, Nooh, was born when he was 182. Nooh lived on for 950 years preaching the message of Allah. Adam, it is claimed, saw four lakh children and grandchildren before he departed from this world.

Idris Reaches Heaven

Idris was a pious man and one of the early prophets of Islam. He was the first man to write with a pen. Allah raised him to a high station. Once when Prophet Muhammad was on ascension, he met Idris in fourth heaven. Allah was so happy with his good deeds that he revealed to him that he would raise him every day the same amount as the deeds of all Adam's children.

Once an angel visited him and said, 'Idris, could you please speak to the angel of death?' Idris agreed and the angel carried him on his wings towards heaven. When they reached the fourth heaven, they met the angel of death who was surprised to see Idris there as he had been commanded

by Allah to seize his soul from the fourth heaven where no human beings lived.

This is what Allah meant when it was said in a Quranic verse, 'And we raised him to a high station'.

Leading the Way

It is said that Allah sent a prophet to all the people in history, beginning with Adam and concluding with Prophet Muhammad. The Prophet was once asked about the number of prophets in all. He replied, 'One hundred and twenty-four thousand.' Not every prophet was a messenger. In fact, only 313 prophets were messengers. The first among them was Adam. Prophet Muhammad himself said, 'Allah created him with His hand, then He breathed into him the soul which He created for him, then He gave him a perfect shape.' And when the Prophet went on ascension or journey to the heavens, he came across Adam in the first heaven who greeted him, 'Welcome to the pious son, and pious Prophet.'

Message of Nooh

Nooh was a Prophet born 126 years after the first Prophet, Adam, passed away. There are others who believe he came ten centuries after Adam. Nooh had a really long life- as long as 950 years. He was born at a time when people had fallen into superstitious practices, worshipping thousands of false gods.

Nooh tried to bring them out of these deeds. He tried his best, but most people did not listen. Only a handful of people believed in his teachings. Nooh was disappointed. He prayed, 'O my people, Worship Allah! You have no God (worthy of worship) other than Him. Truly I fear for you the chastisement of a momentous Day.' Today, the faithful recite a surah of the Quran by the name of Nooh when they are confronted with a difficulty.

Nooh Tries to Rescue People

Nooh told the people around him to worship only Allah. He asked them to fear Allah, and obey him so that their sins could be forgiven. He tried to tell them every day and every night repeatedly. Unfortunately, most people did not listen. So he prayed to Allah, 'O my Lord! I have called my people night and day, but my calling has only increased their aversion. And whenever I have called them, that You might forgive them, they have put their fingers in the ears, and covered themselves up with their clothes, and persisted, and given themselves to arrogance.'

His sole intention was they should worship only one God. He tried to reason with them, saying that Allah had created them in stages, just like heavens. 'Did you not see how Allah had created seven heavens one above the other, and made the moon a light therein and made the sun a lamp?'

His words proved that the sun had its own light while the moon didn't. Yet the people did not listen.

Nooh Is Helped

As most people refused to give up the worship of false gods, Allah sent relief to Nooh. It was revealed to Nooh, 'No more of your people shall believe in you other than those who have already believed, so grieve no longer at their misdeeds. Construct the Ark under Our Eyes and according to Our Revelation, and address Me no further on behalf of those who have been unjust; they shall be drowned (in the Flood).' So Nooh began to construct the Ark and whenever the leaders of his people passed by, they jeered at him.

Nooh kept his patience. Allah's help was near. Soon, the Ark was ready and he was commanded to board it with his followers, his family except his son who did not follow his ideals. Also, there was a pair of each species. The three-deck Ark sailed forth, braving waves as high as mountains. As they were moving, Nooh called out to his son to join him, but the son refused, believing that the mountain will protect him from the flood. Nooh departed saying, 'There is no protector today from Allah's punishment, except that He should have mercy.'

To Each His Own

After the earth had swallowed back its water and the sky had stopped pouring down rains to the earth, Nooh prayed to Allah to rescue his son. 'O my Lord! My son is of my family, and Your promise is true, and You are the Most Just of the Judges.' Allah said, 'O Nooh! He is not of your family. His conduct is unrighteous. So do not ask Me about that of which you have no knowledge. I admonish you lest you should become one of the ignorant!' Nooh sought refuge in Allah, and he descended in peace.

The loss of his son proved that being somebody's son or father is not sufficient for any human being. Everybody has to earn Allah's pleasure with his own good deeds.

Parents Rewarded for Children's Deeds

We often think children are beneficiaries of parents' hard work, their riches, their knowledge. However, Prophet Muhammad said, 'Whoever recited the Quran, studied it, and acted according to what it contains; on the Day of Judgment his parents will be dressed with a crown of light, its brightness is like that of the sun. And his parents will be adorned with two bracelets, of which the whole world is not equivalent to them (in worth). So they will say, Why are we being adorned with these?' It will be said, 'This is because of your child taking (the recitation, teaching and acting upon) the Quran.'

A Commoner Becomes a Prince

Firaun, the king of Egypt, was known to be cruel. When he got to know of any woman delivering a male baby, he would get his soldiers to slay the baby soon after his birth to avoid any future challenger to his throne. He thought this would also weaken his enemies within his kingdom.

When Musa was born, his mother, knowing the impending danger, quickly suckled him, put him in a chest and left it floating on the river. His sister ran alongside as the chest floated away with the river current, till she lost sight of it. While floating down the Nile, it got stuck on the banks. Musa was picked up by Firaun's family. The moment the queen saw the little baby, she fell in love with him and decided to raise him as her own son.

Thus, Musa started growing up in the king's home. The king had no idea it was a child of a commoner and he did not want to make his wife angry. So Musa spent his days in the royal household as a little prince. During this time, it so happened that no midwife in the palace was able to suckle this new born. A regal decision was taken to try Musa's mother who would be ideal for the job. Thus, by the grace of God, Musa was reunited with his birth mother, who was now also his official caretaker!

At Mount Tur

One day, Musa set out with his family from Madyan toward Mount Tur. It was cold and dark. Along the way, he saw some fire in the distance. He asked his family to wait while he went to bring some firewood.

When Musa came close to the fire, he was called from the right side of the valley of Tuwa. It was a divine call. 'O Musa! I am Allah, the Lord of the worlds. Throw down your staff.' The staff soon quivered like a snake. Frightened, Musa ran away. Allah called him back, 'O Musa! Come back and fear not, for you are quite secure. And put your hand into your bosom, and it will come out shining white without stain, and draw your hand close to your side to be free from fear. Those are two proofs from your Lord to Firaun and his chiefs, for indeed they are a wicked people.' The staff and the shining hand were to come to Musa's rescue in Firaun's court.

The story of Musa's journey with his family is recounted in Surah Ta-Ha and Surah An-Naml of the glorious Quran.

Divine Words

Allah chose Musa to spread His Message. As Musa did not have clear speech, his brother Harun was sent along. He asked them not to slacken in their remembrance of Him, as He sent them away to Firaun's land. Firaun was known to be a cruel ruler, brooking no opposition.

Allah, however, instructed Musa to be gentle to him. With these words of Allah, Musa was sent on his mission, 'I was watching you all the time when you were in the palace of Firaun. You were under My Protection and Guardianship. Then I took you out of Egypt to the land of Madyan according to My Plan and your destiny. Then you had to stay therein for some years, and then you came here, O Musa, as decreed. Everything has been happening according to My Plan that I devised for you. Then I have chosen you for My Self (message).'

The instructions were similar to what we are told through Surah Nahl of the glorious Quran, 'Invite (all) to the way of your Lord with wisdom and beautiful preaching and reason with them in ways that are best and most gracious.'

Not Easy for Brothers

Things were not easy for Musa and Harun at the court of Firaun. He was both powerful and intolerant. The two brothers, however, had a mission to fulfil. Fear could not be their ally. So when they met Firaun, he asked, 'And who is your Lord, Musa?' Musa replied, 'Our Lord is He who gave everything its creation and then guided it.'

Firaun was not satisfied. He asked, 'What about the earlier generations?' Musa replied, 'The knowledge of that is with my Lord, in a Book. My Lord never errs, nor forgets. Allah is the One Who had made for you the earth as a cradle, and has opened roads for you therein, and sent down water from the sky.'

Yet again, Firaun rejected Musa's reasoning. He was overcome with pride, and wondered if Musa had come to drive him and his people out.

The Reign of Terror Ends

After Musa had defeated his magicians and sorcerers, King Firaun was angry and decided to put an end to Musa's life for challenging his authority. Musa got to know of it, and decided to save his life along with his followers.

As Firaun's army followed Musa and his followers, they came to the shores of the sea. Allah parted the sea for them so that the believers could go across to dry land on the other shore. As they passed, Allah began folding in the waters behind them, to keep them out of harm's way. When Firaun's army closed in, they were all drowned in the same sea. Firaun too, met a tragic end as a result of his own evil actions. His body is preserved to this day, in the same act of surrender with his arm upwards as the moment of his death.

The Scriptures

Once, Allah called Musa to Him for forty nights. Musa went to Allah and in his absence, left his brother Haroon, to look after affairs. His people, meanwhile, forgot all that Musa had taught them. On his return, Musa was bewildered to find them indulging in extravagance and fawning over a calf. He was angry with his brother, who pleaded helplessness. Musa had taught them to live a life of simplicity, good deeds and remembering God in everyday actions. He was disappointed and asked Allah for help. As a result, Allah gave Musa the Scripture and the criterion for the people to lead a contented, happy and harmonious life. Thus came about the Torah, which according to the Quran, is the first book revealed by Allah.

People Are Pardoned

When Musa was away, his people made out of their ornaments a little calf. When they blew into it, the non-living calf made a sound which resembled that of a cow. They started worshipping the calf, forgetting all that Musa had taught them about not putting anybody at par with Allah. On his return, Musa was so angry to know of the calf worship that he became almost violent with his brother who was helpless in stopping the people. The masses realised their mistake, and sought forgiveness of Allah. They were pardoned, as Allah is merciful and accepting of repentance.

Saved by Faith

Prophet Lut was the nephew of Prophet Ibrahim. He was sent to the people of Palestine, Sodom, and its seven cities to preach the divine message. The cities lay on an important and profitable trade route. The Sodomites used to rob the wayfarers and were a violent lot. They would steal and tell lies. Lut requested them to lead a proper life. Only a few of them listened to him, while most turned a deaf ear.

One day, Allah sent down three guests to Lut's place. As Lut prepared a feast for them, he was worried for their safety. He did not want them to stay over for the night. These guests were actually the angels Jibrail, Mikaeel and Israfeel! They asked Lut to leave the city at night with his followers, leaving behind his wife, who was one of the evil doers who had informed the Sodomites of the presence of the handsome men who they could make ill use of. The Sodomites attacked Lut's house to capture the men to quench their evil desires. They were expecting men, not angels! As soon as Lut left safely with his family, the angels rained brimstones on the Sodomites, bringing them to their end. Among them was Lut's wicked wife, proving yet again that each person bears the burden of his own actions.

Cow Sacrifice

Challenges never ended for Musa. He never buckled down before any of them. If he held his own in front of Firaun, he did not hesitate to help the women looking for water at Madyan or to take his own people to task for worshipping animals. Nor did he spare his brother for their misdeeds. He always related Allah's message to them faithfully. Once he said to his people, 'Allah commands you to slaughter a cow.' They thought he was mocking them. So they started asking a series of questions like 'Ask your Lord to make clear to us what kind it should be,' and 'Ask your Lord for us that He may make clear to us what its colour should

be.' Musa replied patiently that the cow should be neither too old nor too young, and it should be yellow in colour.

Then, convinced of Musa's sincerity, they sacrificed the cow. Once again, Musa's assertiveness and patience saved them from going astray.

No Easy Sacrifice

After they had made a joke of Musa asking them to sacrifice a cow, Allah put a series of tests before the people, before accepting their sacrifice. Like they had asked repeated questions to Musa to almost avoid sacrificing the animal, they had to search far and wide for a cow with yellow skin. Wherever they went, they could not find a cow not too old, not too young, and yellow in colour. Finally, they found one such cow.

They asked the owner to sell the cow to them. He refused. They offered to pay a higher price. Again, to no avail. Then, they offered to pay in gold for the weight of the cow. The man still did not budge. The people became anxious that they may not be able to sacrifice the animal as dictated. So they offered to pay ten times the cow's weight in gold. Upon this, the man agreed. The cow was procured and sacrificed. The people then knew, never to doubt a Prophet or to mock at his teachings.

The Story of Khizr

Khizr was a man of wisdom. He was a man of great insight. Musa wanted to learn from him. Khizr said it was not possible. When Musa assured him that he was a man of patience, he agreed to let Musa travel with him, asking him not to question him until he said so.

As Khizr and Musa went together on a boat, Khizr made a hole in it. Musa said, 'You have done a grievous thing.' Khizr said, 'Did I not say to you that you would not be able to bear with me patiently?' Musa remembered his pledge and sought pardon. They moved on and met a boy who was killed by Khizr. Once again, Musa could not resist saying, 'You have killed an innocent boy who had not killed anybody!' Khizr yet again reminded him of the condition. Musa apologised, 'If I ever question you again about anything after this, then keep me no more with you.'

The two of them reached a town and asked for food. They found none. There they found a wall about to collapse. Khizr restored the wall, leaving Musa asking, 'If you wanted, you could have extracted payment for it.' Khizr thus announced the parting of ways. He said, 'As for the boat, it belonged to the poor men who toiled in the sea. I made it useless, for behind them was a king who was seizing all boats. As for the boy, his parents were believers, and we feared that he would impose upon them insolence. And as for the wall, it belonged to two orphan boys in town. Beneath it was a treasure belonging to them and their father was a righteous man. So your Lord desired that they should attain the age of maturity and bring forth the treasure, a mercy from your Lord.'

The Wells of Madyan

Madyan was an oasis settlement located in the land of Arabia. It was a mystical place around which were desert sands as far as the eye could see. One could see mirages created very often in the dry, scorching heat. There was hardly a tree to shade oneself against the heat away from Madyan. Water was scarce in the desert lands and often travellers and locals ended up quarreling over water from the oasis. Thus, the wells of Madyan became important to all travellers and locals. The boys would bully the girls, making them wait to give drinking water to their animals while those bullies drank their fill. One day, a man helped the girls by taking their sheep and other animals to water. These girls were sisters and being grateful to him, invited him home.

Their old father was very happy on seeing someone help his children and gave the man an offer. He could marry any one of his daughters and stay with him for eight years, looking after his business. After that, he was free to go wherever he wished. The kind man accepted the offer. He married one of the daughters and looked after the old man's sheep. The girls no longer had to worry about going to the well. The old man was Prophet Shuaib and the kind man who helped the girls was none other than Prophet Musa.

Trading with a Conscience

The town of Madyan was a busy business centre. People would bring their produce from far off lands to sell it in Madyan. Honest traders were few and far between. Most would cheat, given half a chance. They would weigh the goods in lesser quantity while selling them at a higher price! They constantly short-changed their customers. Prophet Shuaib, who saw the way business was conducted, was upset with them and urged them to weigh and measure properly. The locals believed that if they traded honestly, they would not make any profit. Cheating had become a way of life for them. Prophet Shuaib pleaded with them to mend their ways. They threatened to banish the prophet if he got in their way. One day, the entire town of Madyan was hit by an earthquake. Not one man was left alive. The entire town was run to the ground, bringing to light the all-seeing nature of Allah's justice.

Prosperity and Greed

Prophet Hud was from the family of prophet Nooh. He lived in Ad, an area of wind-carved sand hills, now modern Yemen and Oman.

The people of Ad were rich and prosperous. They led luxurious lifestyles, building magnificent buildings and lofty mansions. As they prospered, they forgot Allah and continued their pursuit of pleasure endlessly. Hud asked them to lead a compassionate and pious life, sharing their wealth with others. They were greedy and did not heed his advice. Instead, they mocked him. Hud tried pleading but to no avail.

One day, this town was hit by a terrible sandstorm. The storm overtook the town at night and by morning, all houses were buried along with its inhabitants. The mighty city was reduced to a mound of sand. A sprawling city of luxurious living was now nonexistent on the map of Arabia!

Luqman to His Son

Luqman was a wise man and led a pious life, spending his time in prayer. He spoke softly, never raised his voice and treated everybody gently.Luqman was also a caring father who wanted his son to be a good boy with character. He urged him to mind his speech, so that people would not be hurt with what he, said. He reminded his son, 'Do not be arrogant and do not walk with pride. Always keep your voice soft for the harshest of voices is that of a donkey.' For him, a person who screamed in public was like a donkey making ugly noises. He was also a good husband and a sensitive man. He would ask his son not to join others in worship with Allah but instead, spend time in helping his mother that would bring him the same blessings as prayer does. He realised that mothers take great trouble washing ,cleaning and feeding their children selflessly, making sure they grow up with good values. A mother therefore, deserved the highest respect.

Wisdom Has No Age

In ancient Iraq, there was a famous mystic by the name of Junayd Baghdadi. He was particularly fond of one of his students. This student was pious and led his life according to the codes of Islam. The other students, especially some of the older ones, did not like it. One day, they decided to approach the saint with their complaint. Baghdadi heard them patiently. Then he gave a chicken to each student, asking them to slay it only when there was nobody who could see them.

The next day, all the students had obeyed his command, except one. It was his favourite student who, to everyone else's glee, was in trouble!

Baghdadi looked sternly at the crowd and then asked him the reason. The student replied that he tried but could not find a place where nobody looked. Wherever he went, Allah could see him. So, he let the chicken be!

His reply stunned all the students who were sitting in awe of his wisdom. They now knew why he was worthy of being the favourite student of the great saint and congratulated him on his answer!

Diluted Milk

Caliph Umar was renowned for being just. He cared for his people and would take a round of his estate every night to know if everyone was well. On one such round, he heard a conversation between a mother and daughter, on milk. The mother was asking the daughter to dilute milk by adding water to it, to make more profit than they could hope to make by selling the milk as it was. She wanted her to finish the job in the darkness of the night, away from prying eyes.

The daughter refused to do so. She had integrity of character and quoted the Caliph's stand on such an action. The mother was bent on making more profit. So she replied that the Caliph is unlikely to see her at night. Upon this the daughter replied, 'If the Caliph is not seeing us, then the Almighty will surely see us.'

The Caliph overheard this conversation. He was so impressed with the young woman's honesty and strength of character that he, soon, asked his son to marry her. The young woman's fate changed overnight from poor to rich, all because she stood for what was right. The Caliph lived his days contentedly with his son and worthy daughter-in-law, in a home filled with the love and care that this young woman had created. The value of good character is indeed, priceless !

33

Pride Comes Before a Fall

The people of Thamud used to live in the Southern Peninsula of Arabia but soon moved northwards to Mount Athlab. They were probably successors of Ad who used to stay not too far from that place earlier. They inherited the mansions in the plains and many palaces of Ad. There was a man among them who did not like their ways. He advised them strongly against indulging in corrupt practices. He told them not to equate anybody with Allah in worship and to avoid cheating as Allah was always watching.

The people of Thamud were not convinced. They asked him for proof. Allah provided this pious man with a she-camel as a sign from Him. The people were told to let her eat and drink and not restrain the animal. The locals decided to tie down the animal and challenged this pious man. Soon, an earthquake hit them, leaving the township as barren as a dry twig.

It is believed that the man who tried taking them to a better life but failed as they did not take his advice, was the great Prophet Salih.

Saving the Innocent

Abraha was a Yemenese king who had an ambition to conquer great lands. One of his ambitions was to destroy the Kaaba and take control of the territory. The local people there led simple lives and could not match up to the strength of Abraha's intended invasion. The day arrived soon. The king came with an army of 60,000 troops and a herd of 13 giant war elephants. He marched towards the Kaaba, confident that he had already won the land. His opponents were weak and had no such powerful army. Along the way whosoever resisted him was either killed or taken as a prisoner or was made a guide for the expedition. As the troops marched from Yemen to Arabia with nothing but destruction on their minds, Allah saved the peaceloving local men and women in a wonderful way! A massive flock of birds

flew over the elephants and the troops, carrying in their beaks sharp-edged hard stones. As the shower of stones rained down, the invaders were either killed or dispersed in no time, never to return. Thus, the Kabbah and the area around it was saved by the grace of Allah and the peaceful and godly men and women continued to enjoy their way of life.

Ibrahim Wonders

As a little boy, Lut's uncle, Ibrahim, sat on a sand dune gazing at the night sky and wondered about the magic of the night. He admired the night sky and saw a bright star twinkling beautifully in the darkness. He thought the star was his god. Then it faded away. He thought to himself, that which fades away cannot be god. Then he saw the moon shimmering with its sparkling beauty. He thought that would be his god. But the moon too had to set. Ibrahim felt that, that which sets cannot be his god. Come dawn, he saw the sun rising in all its glory. He wanted to believe that the sun was his god. But then came the evening and the sun set, leaving Ibrahim to realise that one that

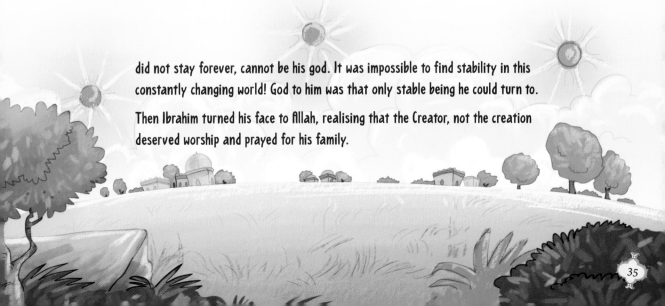

did not stay forever, cannot be his god. It was impossible to find stability in this constantly changing world! God to him was that only stable being he could turn to.

Then Ibrahim turned his face to Allah, realising that the Creator, not the creation deserved worship and prayed for his family.

Babylon's Idols

The Babylon people loved their idols. They served them food and worshipped them sincerely. They would have an annual festival to celebrate, which was a sight to be seen and people from all across the land would be invited to days of merry celebration.

On one such occasion, Ibrahim decided to stay and wait. After all the people had left after a night of gluttonous merriment, Ibrahim went up to the idols placed in a magnificent room with lots of food on offer. He wondered why the gods did not eat such lovely food! He smashed the smaller idols with an axe, leaving the axe in the hands of the biggest idol.

When the residents came back, they were horrified. They asked, 'Who has done this?' Ibrahim was asked the question too. He replied, 'It was the biggest of them that did it. So ask (him)'. The residents looked at him and replied, 'Surely, you know that they do not speak.' This was the moment Ibrahim had been waiting for. 'Do you worship what you yourself have fashioned out of your own hands?' he asked. What he meant was that the Creator alone was worthy of worship, not something that we fashion out of our own hands.

Test by Fire

The villagers were angry with Ibrahim for he had broken their idols, a symbol of their faith. They decided to prepare a huge fire and throw him into it. Men and women started gathering wood from every corner of the town.

Ibrahim was tied in chains and placed on a catapult. As he was being thrown into the fire, he prayed to Allah one last time. Angel Jibrail wanted to help. Ibrahim refused. As the fire was lit, Allah's command came. He said, 'O fire! Be cool and safe for Ibrahim.' The fire roared and burnt the chains with which Ibrahim was shackled without touching an inch of his body. Ibrahim remained safe.

Bearing Miracles

One day, Ibrahim sat at home with his old wife Sara. They were preparing for dinner at home. Just then, three guests arrived at their place. Ibrahim and Sara were surprised to receive them at that late an hour. Ibrahim welcomed them and invited them to have dinner with them. The guests however, did not extend their hands towards the food. As Ibrahim insisted that they must try out the food, they disclosed their identity. They told him, they were angels who had been sent to the people of Lut and to give good news to Ibrahim that he will soon be blessed with a son.

Ibrahim was surprised. They had no children though they had been married for long. Sara exclaimed, 'What wonder! How shall I bear a child now when I am an old woman and my husband is an old man? That would be an unusual thing.' The angels assured her that it would happen, saying, "Do you wonder at Allah's decree?"

Soon their glad tidings came true. Ibrahim and his wife were blessed with a son. They named him Ismail, also known as Ishaq. Sara and Ibrahim were very happy. Their long cherished desire to be parents was fulfilled. They had a son to share their lives with.

Construction of the Kaaba

Allah commanded Ibrahim and Ismail to build the House of Worship at Bakka, which later came to be known as Makkah. Initially, the two of them did not know where to build it. Then, Allah sent a wind called Al-Khajuj, which had two wings and a head in the shape of a snake. The wind cleared the area around the Kaaba. Lo and behold! As the desert sands disappeared, they revealed the old foundations of the house of worship to Ibrahim and Ismail. When they completed the foundation, Ibrahim asked his son to get him the choicest selection of rock to be laid there. That is when angel Jibrail brought him the Black Stone. The sins of Adam's progeny had turned it black. When Ismail returned with a stone that he found, he was surprised to see the Black Stone. He asked his father about who had brought it. Ibrahim replied, "It was brought by one who never gets tired.'It was the angel Jibrail who had helped build it.

Thus the construction started. When the House of Worship was completed, Ibrahim gratefully prayed, "Our Lord! Accept this from us; surely You are the All-hearing, All-knowing."

An Honest Neighbour

Abu Dajanah always used to pray right behind where the Prophet would bow and pray. However, as soon as the prayer was over, he would be the first to come out of the mosque. He would never hang around for small chat with the companions of the Prophet or even stay on to seek Allah's blessing at the conclusion of the prayer.

This caught the eye of the Prophet. One day he asked him, 'O, Abu Dajanah, don't you need anything from Allah?'

Abu Dajanah replied, 'O Messenger of Allah, Yes I do. I can't live without Allah even for as long as the blink of an eye.'

The Prophet said, 'So why don't you stay with us after prayers and ask Allah what you need?'

To this Abu Dajanah replied, ' I have a Jewish neighbour who has a date tree and its branches extend into the courtyard of my house. When the wind blows at night, the dates fall into my courtyard. That is why I rush from the mosque and collect the dates to return them to the owner before my kids wake up; because once they wake up, they will eat them, as they are hungry. One day, I saw one of my children chewing a date and I took it out with my finger before he could swallow it. When my son cried, I said to him, 'Aren't you ashamed of standing in front of Allah as a thief?'

A companion of the Prophet, Abu Bakr, known to be a well-off man, heard about Abu Dajanah's situation. He went to the house of the Jewish man and bought the date tree from him, gifting it to Abu Dajanah and his family.

When the Jewish man learned the truth of the matter, he was so impressed with Abu Dajanah's honesty that he went to the Prophet and announced his intention to embrace Islam. Abu Dajanah had proved to be a living example of an honest neighbour as a believer of Islam.

Dhul-Kifl

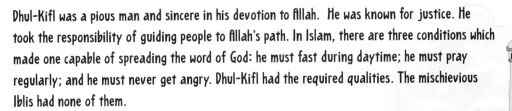

Dhul-Kifl was a pious man and sincere in his devotion to Allah. He was known for justice. He took the responsibility of guiding people to Allah's path. In Islam, there are three conditions which made one capable of spreading the word of God: he must fast during daytime; he must pray regularly; and he must never get angry. Dhul-Kifl had the required qualities. The mischievious Iblis had none of them.

Dressed as an old man, he came up to Dhul-Kifl at the time of his afternoon nap. He claimed his people were unjust towards him. Dhul-Kifl heard his long story and told him to come to the court. The old man did not show up. Next afternoon, when Dhul-Kifl was about to rest, the old man came again, claiming he had been cheated. Dhul-Kifl invited him to the court again. The old man did not turn up. Yet again, at the siesta time, he turned up at Dhul-Kifl's place. The guard denied him entry this time. So he climbed up the roof and came to Dhul-Kifl, confident that Dhul-Kifl would get angry. However, he remained at peace. He saw through the facade and questioned, 'Are you an enemy of Allah?' Iblis realised he had been found out and confessed. To this day, anger is seen as the work of Shaitan in Islam.

Prayers in a Mosque

Once, a companion of the Prophet asked him about different mosques. He wanted to know the name of the first mosque ever built. The Prophet replied that it was Al-Masjid Al-Haram or the Sacred Mosque at Makkah. The follower egged on, 'Which was the next mosque ever built after that?' The Prophet said, 'Al-Masjid Al-Aqsa.' The Prophet mentioned that there were forty years between the constructions of the two mosques.

The companion continued on his query on the next mosque. The Prophet saw through his curiosity and answered his actual question. 'Wherever you are, at the time of prayer, you can pray, because Allah is everywhere.' Any place can be holy to pray as long as it is a clean place and one is not inconveniencing others while offering prayers in that place.

The Power of Dreams

Yaqub had twelve sons, out of which Yusuf was the most devoted, handsome and disciplined. One night, Yusuf saw eleven stars, the sun and the moon in his dream. They looked like they were bowing to him. He wondered what the dream was all about. His father told him not to relate his dream to his jealous brothers as they might try to harm him. He further assured him that the Lord would help him understand the symbols of his dream if he had patience. Yusuf agreed and waited. Soon the day came when the Lord helped him interpret his dream through his thoughts.

The dream was clear. Eleven stars meant his eleven brothers. The sun and the moon stood for Yusuf's parents. And all of them prostrating to him meant he would rise high in life, so much so, that even his parents would respect and honour him. Yusuf's dream proved correct many years later when he became a prophet revered by all.

Twist of Fate

Yusuf's brothers were jealous of him because he was their father's favourite. All, except the little Binyameen. Yusuf was fond of him, just as his father was fond of Yusuf. The other brothers often devised plans to get rid of Yusuf. One day, they sought their father's permission to take Yusuf out with them. When they assured him that they would look after him, he relented. The brothers made an evil plan to throw little Yusuf into a well. The plan took shape. The brothers came back home in the evening to tell their father that Yusuf had been eaten by a wolf. To assure him, they showed him a shirt stained with blood.

Their father did not believe them. He kept his patience. Many years passed and there was no word about Yusuf. The father had faith that Yusuf was alive and one day, he will come back to him as a handsome young man. He prayed to Allah all the time. His patience was rewarded many years later when it was discovered that Yusuf was hale and hearty. Though thrown into the well, he had been rescued by a passing caravan going to Egypt. He was brought up by a rich minister in Egypt. Little Yusuf grew up with all the luxuries while his brothers toiled every day for their bread, even though they had wished the worst for him.

Yusuf Is Attacked

Yusuf grew up to be a good looking, wise man. He remained grateful to the minister who brought him up like a son. The minister's wife, unfortunately, wanted him to be her partner. Yusuf remembered the kindness of the minister. He could not let the kind man down. Yusuf thus, decided to run away. The minister's wife ran after him, and pulled at his shirt to stop him from running out. The minister happened to be standing at the doorstep at the time. Seeing him, she accused Yusuf of being a bad man. A witness was called for. Yusuf defended himself. The minister commanded that if the shirt was torn from the front, the minister's wife was speaking the truth. If it was torn from the back, then Yusuf was speaking the truth. The shirt was examined by the minister. It was torn from the back. It was thus proved that Yusuf was a man of integrity who was grateful to the minister for bringing him up.

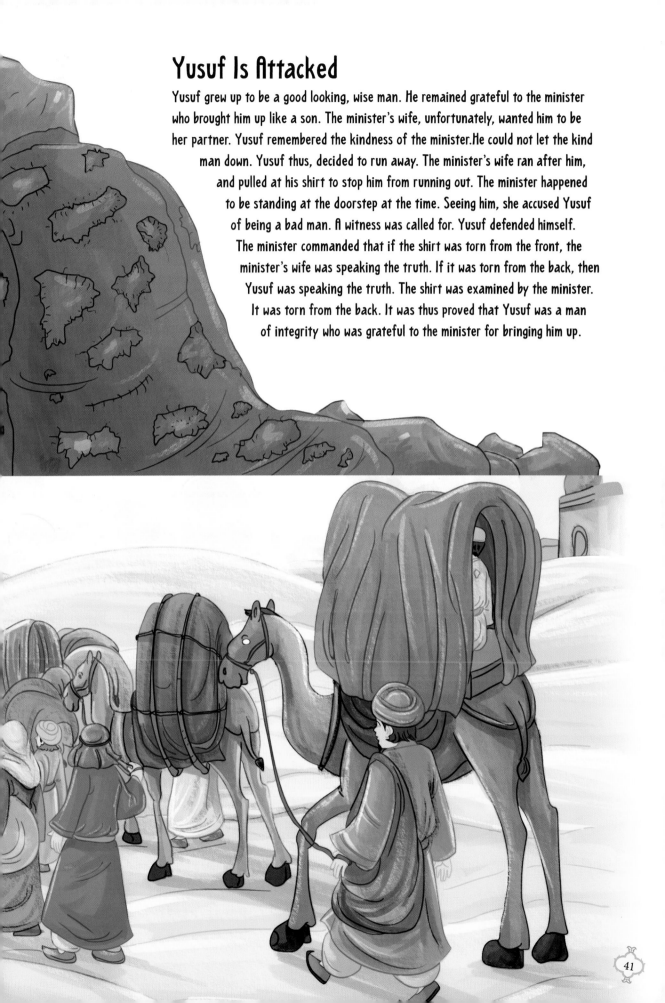

A Handsome Man

As years passed, Yusuf turned from a little boy to a handsome young man. He was said to have half of the beauty of the world. It was no surprise that the minister's wife started getting close to him. Soon, everybody in the town knew about the minister's wife's fascination.

She wanted her respect back. She was certain that if any woman saw Yusuf, she would fall in love with him. One day, she threw a big party and invited all her friends. She prepared a grand feast for them. She was clever. Once the main course was over, she gave each woman separate dishes of fruits with a knife each, to cut them.

Then she asked for Yusuf, who was clad in new, attractive clothing, to be brought before the guests. One look at him and all the women ended up nicking their hands without immediately realising the pain.

The minister's wife told them, 'This was the man for whom you blamed me.'

Yusuf was put into prison so that women could be away from him. It was in prison that he was to learn the most important lessons of life that proved useful when he went on to be a minister himself.

Two Dreams

Yusuf was no ordinary prisoner. He was a gifted and devout man who could interpret dreams. Often, prisoners, and even those from the world outside, came to relate their dreams to him. Yusuf was happy to interpret the meaning of their dreams. Once, two prisoners came to him. Each had seen a dream. One of them narrated to Yusuf that he had seen himself pressing wine in his dream. The other dreamed that he was carrying bread on his head from which the birds were eating.

Yusuf pondered over the meaning of their dreams. Then he came to a conclusion: the one pressing wine was told he would pour out wine for his master. It meant he would rise in life and move around with powerful people. The one carrying bread was told he would be crucified and the birds shall eat from his head. Yusuf had only one request to the cup-bearer or wine presser. 'Mention me to your master,' he requested. When the cup-bearer was released, he, unfortunately, forgot it for the longest time.

Fortune Teller

The king of Egypt had a dream. He called all the religious men to interpret it for him. They failed. Then one of them remembered Yusuf and his ability to interpret dreams. The king called for Yusuf and narrated to him his dream, in which he had seen seven fat cows and seven lean cows that were devouring them. He saw seven green ears of corn and seven withered ones. Yusuf understood the context and told the king, 'For seven years, you shall sow continuously without a break. Then what you get of that harvest, you would need to store, except that which you need to eat. Soon after, there will be seven years in which you shall devour what you reserved in the good years. After that will come a good year when there will be rain and people will press wine.' He identified seven years of good harvest followed by seven years of drought. The king realised that Yusuf was a wise man and released him, making him a minister in his court that day.

Reuniting with Binyameen

Yusuf was responsible for Egypt's treasuries. He knew that drought was round the corner, so food had to be rationed. One day, his ten elder brothers came to buy food from him. Yusuf was thirty years old. He had not seen them since he was a child when they had thrown him in a well, wishing him dead out of jealousy. They could not recognise him now. He asked about their eleventh brother, telling them to bring him along next time without which he would not give them their food grains. Quietly, he asked his assistants to keep their money back in the sacks loaded on their camels.

On reaching home, the brothers asked their father for permission to carry their youngest brother Binyameen with them. The father agreed and they went to buy the grain from Yusuf with Binyameen, which he gave. He was thankful to be reunited to his youngest brother who had been blameless in the conspiracy. Allah had yet again reunited him with his kin!

The Golden Bowl

While Yusuf entertained his other evil brothers, he quietly placed a golden bowl in Binyameen's bag. His family, from whom he was separated for years, had assumed he was dead, which left his innocent brother, Binyameen and his father grieving. Yusuf could not have made innocent Binyameen stay back officially, as he was a minister. This was not the right time to reveal his identity to the two. All the brothers were fed, as was the royal decorum. Just then a herald announced that the king's drinking bowl was missing. The one with the bowl would be held back; the rest could leave. All the bags were checked and the bowl was found in Binyameen's bag. Yusuf's brothers went back home afraid of their father, as they had left the youngest one behind. Meanwhile, at the palace, Yusuf got the privacy to reunite with his dear brother Binyameen, who was overjoyed at the turn of events!

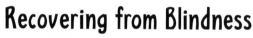

Recovering from Blindness

Yusuf's brothers returned, relating the incident to their father. He couldn't trust their story due to their previous lies that parted Yusuf from him. He knew that it wasn't the truth and this opened the father's eyes! He cried endlessly for his two beloved sons, Yusuf and Binyameen. As he wept, he lost his eyesight.

The blind father now called his sons and asked them to find their two missing brothers. They were confused as they thought that Yusuf was dead. They, however, had to obey their father and went to the minister, pleading for Binyameen's case. At that moment, Yusuf showed up and asked them if they remembered what they did to Yusuf many years ago. The brothers were shocked. They asked, 'Are you indeed Yusuf?' It was then that Yusuf revealed his true identity. They were mortified and confessed their sins, asking for forgiveness for the sake of their blind father. Yusuf gave them his shirt, asking them to cast it over their father's face. This would help to recover his eyesight, he assured them. The brothers did as asked and their old father regained his eyesight instantly!

Fulfilled Prophecy

When Yusuf's father Yaqub recovered his eyesight, he wanted to see his long lost son immediately. So, he went to Egypt with his wife and sons. As they covered the desert and reached the border of Egypt, Yusuf came to receive them, welcoming them to the land where he held a high rank. He took them home and asked them to be seated on resplendant thrones. His parents and all eleven brothers bowed before him in respect. He hugged his father and brothers. That moment was the fulfillment of the dream he had seen many years ago where he saw eleven stars, the sun and the moon bowing to him. When Yaqub died, he asked his sons to follow Islam. Yusuf got his body embalmed for 40 days as a mark of respect for the old man who had been like the sun in his life.

Braveheart

Daud was a man of great strength and was known to be fearless. Allah had made him so powerful that he could often soften the iron with his bare hands. He needed no axe, no hammer and no fire to do the job! Allah taught him the skills of making armour. He would make coats of mail and set the link in even measure, to perfection. In contrast, was his humble devotion to Allah and a compassionate heart for the people. He had such a beautiful voice that when he sang the praises of the Lord, mountains and birds echoed praises of Him. He would fast and eat in moderation. Allah considered him one of His chosen ones for, even though he was strong, he was gentle. He believed in kindness and would stand up with all his might for what was just and fair. Daud's life was his prayer and is, thus, an inspiration to us till date.

Deliverance

The people of Mosul had been irreverent to the prophet's advice to lead a pious life. Yunus decided to leave his people and boarded a ship to go away from the town. The journey started with clear skies and calm waters as the ship sailed through the seas. The ship reached the ocean and soon a storm started brewing. The ship swayed violently in the choppy waves. With too much weight on board and only basic necessities with no land in sight for miles, a tough decision had to be made. The travellers decided to draw lots. Whosoever had his name called out, would be thrown into the waters. Alas, it was Yunus whose name was called out. The travellers, by then, had become fond of Yunus and couldn't see him go and so decided to have another draw. His name turned up again and so, for the sake of the survival of the rest, he was thrown into the ocean. As he tried coming up for air, he was swallowed by a huge whale.

As Yunus settled inside the whale's body, he prayed to Allah fervently. His prayer was answered. Allah knew Yunus to have immense faith. He commanded the whale not to eat Yunus. Not only did he remain unharmed within the belly of the whale, he could hear the voice of the whale glorifying Allah and see the pebbles it had swallowed. He felt at peace and started praying to Allah in complete darkness, 'There is no God but You. Glorfied be You!'

As he prayed, the whale changed direction to the shore and gently spat him out at the shoreline. Yunus knew then that Allah had heard him and was with him every moment of every day!

Gentleness and Strength

One day, two chieftains got into a brawl. The two squared each other. Jalut, the wicked one, challenged Talut (also known as Saul) to come forward and fight him. Nobody rose to the challenge. Saul announced that if anybody from his people stepped forward to challenge Jalut and defeated him, he would give him his daughter in marriage.

Then Daud, a short man with blue eyes, little hair and a big heart, stepped forward. Against all odds, he killed the mighty Jalut. The people were so thrilled with his victory that he was appointed their king for he was kind as he was strong and looked after the welfare of the people. Later, he became the first man in history to be both a prophet and a king.

Value of Life

Suleman was the most gifted of rulers. He inherited Daud's prophethood and also his kingdom. He was given huge armies of men, djinns, wild animals and birds. He understood the science of matter as well. He could understand the speech of the animals and of the ants. He could converse with birds too. One day, he marched with his army to a valley. An ant saw the army approaching and alerted the other ants to go away to their dwellings as they could be crushed. Suleman understood what she said and waited till the ants were safe. He was grateful for his gift as he did not want to kill innocent beings. He thanked Allah for all the favours conferred upon him and went on with his journey soon after, to the joy of the ants who blessed him.

Every Being Is Unique

One day, Suleman on an inspection, found his hoopoe bird missing. He was worried and warned the bird that he would punish it unless it came up with an acceptable reason for absence. Soon, the hoopoe arrived with news from Sheba.

Suleman kept his anger in check as the bird was crucial to his intelligence operations at that time. The hoopoe also had the ability to detect a source of water and its flow from the underbelly of the earth. On Suleman's long, arduous travels, once the hoopoe discovered water, Suleman's vast army would dig the earth and find water to quench everybody's thirst. The bird was essential for his men to reach the land of Sheba, as living without water over long distances was impossible. Sometimes, the smallest being can be of the greatest help if one does not underestimate living beings and their potential!

The Crystal Palace

The Hoopoe bird gave news about the queen of Sheba to Suleman. The queen was known as Bilqis and worshipped the sun. She had a magnificent throne. Hearing the news, Suleman sent a letter through the bird to the queen. She read out the letter which asked her to submit to Suleman. The queen consulted her ministers and sent Suleman a gift in return. Suleman asked her ambassador, 'Are you sending us wealth? But what Allah has bestowed on me is better than what He has bestowed on you.' Suleman threatened to send his vast army to her kingdom. The queen had no choice but to surrender. Suleman even got the djinns to bring over her throne. Suleman showed her a crystal glass palace with streams of water where there were fish. Thinking it was water, she uncovered her legs to walk. It was then, that Suleman told her it wasn't water but crystal glass! Awed at these miracles, Bilqis turned to Suleman's faith.

God Willing

Suleman wanted to sire sons to work in the path shown by Allah and wanted to spread the word of Allah far and wide. One day, he declared that he would take on a hundred women to conceive children the very same night.

However, none of the women, except one, conceived. The baby who was delivered was deformed. Everybody was shocked. It is then that Suleman realised that while making the proclamation about siring a hundred sons, he had forgotten Allah. He had forgotten to add in his speech 'If Allah wills so' for any deed is accomplished only if the Lord wills.

Blessed with a Miracle

Imran was a pious man and hailed from the family of Daud. His wife Hannah was a righteous woman. She did not have a child. One day, when she saw a bird feeding its baby, Hannah felt the pangs for a child of her own and promised Allah that she would dedicate the baby to His service if she could have one. Soon, Allah blessed her with a baby.

Hannah was overjoyed and prayed to Allah, 'My Lord! I have dedicated to You what is in my womb as a holy gift, so please accept this from me.' When the baby was born, she named her Maryam and commanded her and her off-spring in the protection of Allah, away from the tricks of Iblis.

Maryam grew up to be a woman of exceptional beauty and purity in her own right and is revered in the verses of the Quran.

The Draw of Lots

It is said that at the time of birth, Satan touches the baby, so the baby howls. Allah made only two exceptions to this rule as these two children were exceptionally special.

Maryam, and later, Maryam's son, Isa were not kicked by Satan and so these were the only two humans who did not howl at birth. As they were special, they had to be taken care of well. The Lord had a plan.

When Isa was to be born, Maryam was taken care of at the mosque as she was the daughter of the Imam and was very popular. Each person wanted to take care of her so there was a draw of lots. Interestingly, there were so many well-wishers of Maryam that people had three draws to find the name of the caretaker. The people collected their pens and asked a child to pick one. Zakariya, the prophet, won. They, then, threw the pens into the river and opted to pick one flowing against the current. Zakariya won again. Finally, they had the third draw, throwing their pens into the river and choosing the pen which went with the flow. Zakariya's pen emerged the victor. Thus, Zakariya came to be the chosen one.

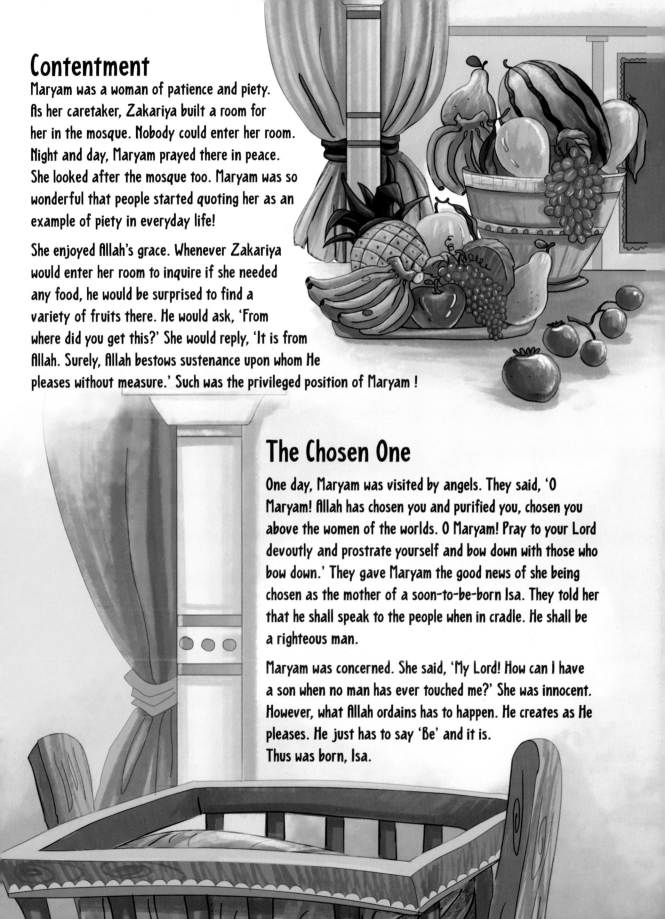

Contentment

Maryam was a woman of patience and piety. As her caretaker, Zakariya built a room for her in the mosque. Nobody could enter her room. Night and day, Maryam prayed there in peace. She looked after the mosque too. Maryam was so wonderful that people started quoting her as an example of piety in everyday life!

She enjoyed Allah's grace. Whenever Zakariya would enter her room to inquire if she needed any food, he would be surprised to find a variety of fruits there. He would ask, 'From where did you get this?' She would reply, 'It is from Allah. Surely, Allah bestows sustenance upon whom He pleases without measure.' Such was the privileged position of Maryam !

The Chosen One

One day, Maryam was visited by angels. They said, 'O Maryam! Allah has chosen you and purified you, chosen you above the women of the worlds. O Maryam! Pray to your Lord devoutly and prostrate yourself and bow down with those who bow down.' They gave Maryam the good news of she being chosen as the mother of a soon-to-be-born Isa. They told her that he shall speak to the people when in cradle. He shall be a righteous man.

Maryam was concerned. She said, 'My Lord! How can I have a son when no man has ever touched me?' She was innocent. However, what Allah ordains has to happen. He creates as He pleases. He just has to say 'Be' and it is.
Thus was born, Isa.

51

Isa Tells it All

Isa is referred to as Maryam's son throughout the Quran. His was a unique birth as it was without the intervention of a man. He was the last Israeli prophet. Isa had uncommon gifts. He could cure the sick, the blind and, more importantly, people with leprosy, which was a major cause of death at that time. He could even revive the dead and was blessed with rare knowledge. He talked of the coming of Muhammad, the last prophet. He gave many signs on how to recognise him that had been revealed to him exclusively.

He told the people that the last prophet would be unlettered and would hail from the Arabs. People were surprised as they thought the next prophet too would be from the native people. Isa stated that the name of the next prophet will be Ahmad. This finds mention in their scriptures- the Torah and the Gospel. He would join the good and forbid what was wrong. His words rang true nearly six hundred years later when Muhammad was born in 570 A.D.

The Grace of Ramadan

When Prophet Muhammad was born, Allah ensured that the prestige of every preceding prophet was respected. Thus, He made it mandatory that anybody who believed in Muhammad as the last messenger, had to believe in every prophet or messenger sent before him from Adam to Isa. The Quran, which was revealed in the month of Ramadan tells its believers as much.

Incidentally, all the revered books were revealed in the month of Ramadan. All the dates of revelation came in multiples of six. Thus, the Torah, held as a sacred book by the Jews, was revealed on the 6th day of Ramadan. Zabur, another book of revelations, came on the 12th day of Ramadan, 482 years after the Torah. The Gospel was revealed on the 18th day of Ramadan. The Quran, as many scholars tell us, came with a condition that the faithful had to respect all prophets alike. This holy book was revealed on the 24th day of Ramadan.

The Quran for the Living

The Quran is a book of guidance for the living. It is not a book for the dead. Yet when somebody dies, people tend to call a local cleric and students from a madrasa in the vicinity for Quran khwani or recitation of the Quran. The idea is that the reward for their recitation shall reach the dead. It is not true. Nowhere in the Prophet's time do we come across an instance of Quran khwani. Instead, the Prophet encouraged each one to read the holy book every day, even if it was a small portion, and to think about its message, introspect and ask questions. He encouraged people to clear their doubts. We are told in verse 24 of Surah Muhammad, 'Then do they not reflect upon the Quran, or are there locks upon (their) hearts?'

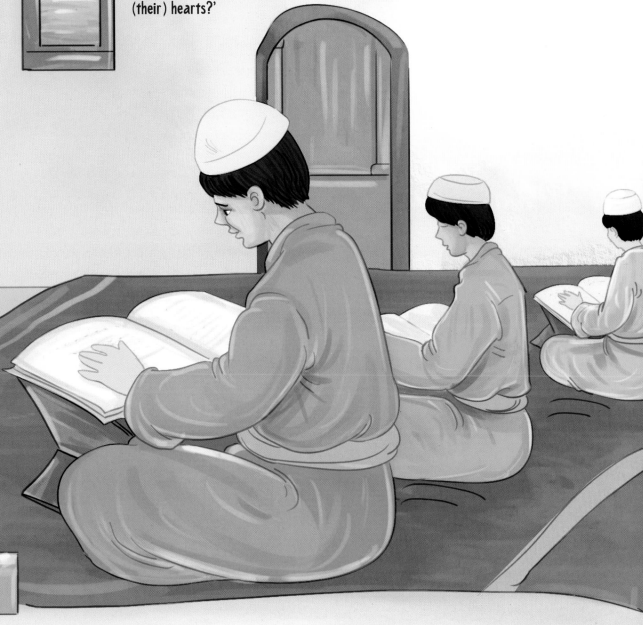

Miswak Benefits

Using miswak (tooth stick made of a tree's stem) to clean one's teeth is considered a sunnah. In fact, it is considered one of the sunnahs to perform before Friday prayers. The Prophet is reported to have said, 'Purify (clean) your mouths with the miswak for indeed it (the mouth) is the pathway of the Quran.'

Showing the Way

The last Messenger of Allah said, 'Any one who shows the path to something good has the same reward as the one who does it.' Indeed, in another Hadith, even giving directions to somebody lost on the road is considered an act of charity for which one would be compensated on the Day of Judgement.

Breathing Life into Birds

Isa was a healer. Not only was he a prophet and a messenger, he was given a divine revelation. Born without the intervention of a father, Isa was given the rarest qualities which any man could aspire for. From his cradle, he could speak to people. From there, he invited people to the path of Allah. He was given powers of creating miracles too. He could bring the dead back to life, heal the sick and give eyesight to the blind. He could create out of clay, a bird and breathe life into it. And lo! It would become a real bird.

He said to his people, 'I have come to you with a sign from your Lord. I make for you out of clay a figure of a bird and I breathe into it, and it becomes a bird by Allah's Permission, and I heal those born blind and the lepers, and I quicken the dead by Allah's Permission, and I inform you of what you eat and what you store up in your houses.'

Abundance from Heaven

Once upon a time, Isa's disciples fasted for a whole month. After they had finished fasting for thirty days, they asked Isa to ask Allah to provide for them, a table full of good food from heaven. Through it they wanted to know if Allah had accepted their fast or not. They wanted to mark the completion of their fast with a day of celebration for all. Isa asked them not to make such a demand. When they insisted, he prayed to Allah to provide them a table full of good food. Allah granted his request and soon a spread of food was laid before Isa's eyes. There were platters full of fruits, seven pieces of fish and seven loafs of bread. Isa asked his disciples to eat to their heart's content. They refused to eat before he tasted it. Isa then asked the poor, the sick and the disabled to help themselves. When they ate, they were all cured of their illnesses. Those who had refused regretted their decision.

This incident of a table full of food finds mention in Surah Maida of the Glorious Quran.

The Ungrateful

The table from heaven was a spread of medicinal food to cure the ill, feed the poor and make the destitute feel loved. It would come once a day and everybody would partake of the food. Some 7,000 people ate at the table every day. Then the table started appearing every alternate day. Only the poor and the needy could eat at it. People became angry at this. They started blaming Isa. They spoke ill of him. Allah decided to put a stop to it altogether. All those who spoke out against Isa were transformed into pigs. This was the punishment for speaking badly against the compassionate prophet. Indeed, Allah said in the Quran, 'I will send it down to you (table spread of food on Isa's prayer), but if any of you disbelieves thereafter, I will chastise him with a chastisement with which I have chastised no one among all people.'

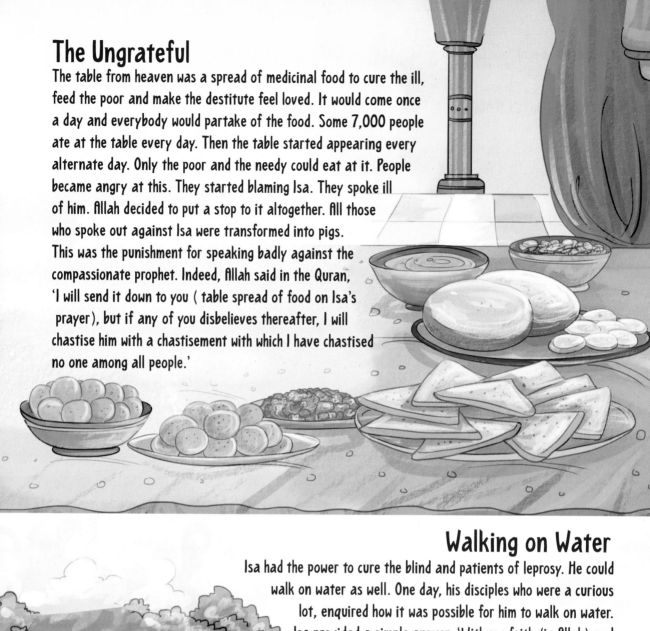

Walking on Water

Isa had the power to cure the blind and patients of leprosy. He could walk on water as well. One day, his disciples who were a curious lot, enquired how it was possible for him to walk on water. Isa provided a simple answer, 'With my faith (in Allah) and certainty.' The disciples decided to follow suit. They claimed to have faith too and as they went deeper into the water they started drowning. They were frightened of the waves. Isa rescued them and asked, 'Do you not fear the Lord of the Waves?' The disciples were silent.

After he rescued them, he took some dust from the earth. When he opened his hands in front of the disciples, one hand had gold, the other some pebbles. He asked the disciples to choose between the two. When they chose gold, he replied, 'They are the same to me.'

Isa's faith did not differentiate between various forms of water! It was constant, whether turbulent or still.

Simple Living

For all his ability to heal the sick, and revive the dead, Isa was a simple man. He had no home, no family and no wealth. He wore woollen clothes and survived on the earnings of his mother Maryam, who used to make yarn. Yet he was known as a great man!

He advised his disciples to live a simple life, and to stay in this world without greed. But they would often follow their vain desires rather than spend their time pursuing knowledge which required them to be simple and thoughtful in their ideas and manner. He would say, 'The sweetness of this world is the bitterness of the Hereafter and the bitterness of this world is the sweetness of the Hereafter. Allah's true followers do not live in luxury. The worst of you is a scholar who gives preference to his desires over his knowledge.'

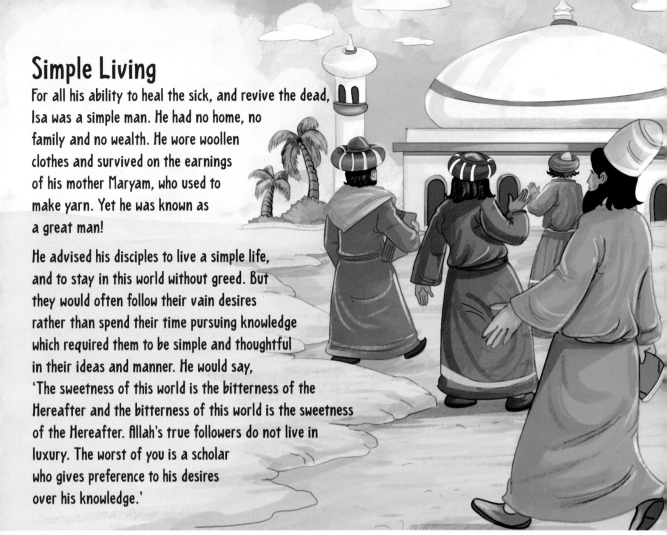

Mindfulness

We often think of crying as a sign of weakness. Boys are told, 'Big boys do not cry.' Isa was different. To him, crying was a sign of piety. He would often advise his disciples to think of the Day of Judgment when everybody will be held to account for his deeds on earth. It would bring tears to the eyes of all, including Isa.

Isa would say, 'O weak son of Adam! Live in this world like a guest, and take the mosques as your home, and teach your eyes to cry and your body to endure, and your heart to reflect. Do not worry about tomorrow's provision because it is a sin.'

Isa lived life in the moment and wanted us to do the same.

The Rising

Isa asked people to worship Allah. He asked them to give up any false gods and not to draw any association between Allah and him, as Allah is the One and only worthy of worship. Most people rejected his teachings. However, some people believed him and became pious followers. They tried to help him to spread the message of Allah.

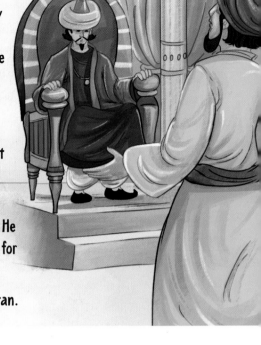

The enemies of Isa were disturbed. They lied to their king about Isa, giving false information as they wanted to get rid of him. Allah, however, had other plans.

Before they could crucify Isa, Allah took him up to Himself. And He put Isa's resemblance on another man. The people mistook him for Isa and crucified him.

The incident is mentioned in Surah Al-Imran of the glorious Quran.

Imbibing the Likeness

When Isa was about to be raised to heaven, he went to meet his companions. They were twelve of them. He took a bath before meeting them. With water still dribbling from his head, he asked them, 'Who from among you will take my likeness and be killed in my place, so will reach my rank?' A young man volunteered. Isa asked him to sit down and repeated the question. Again, the same man raised his hand. Then Isa agreed that he was the one. The likeness of Isa was given to him while Isa was lifted through the window to heaven. Soon, the miscreants came looking for him. They mistook the man who now had the likeness of Isa as Isa himself and they put a crown of thorns over his head just to mock him and after torture, killed him.

This man lost his life to save the prophet and so raised himself to Isa's level!

Isa to Come Back

Muslims believe that one day, Isa will come back to earth. He will come down from heaven and people will recognise him. His head will still be dripping with water. He will descend on the white minaret in Damascus. He will offer Fajr (dawn) prayers there. He will guide the people to godliness. Allah will destroy Dajjal at the hands of Isa.

There will be peace all over again. There will be no wars, no battles. Everybody will live in harmony. No country will attack another country, no tribe will fight with another tribe. It will be a time when camels and lions shall roam around together. It will be a time when tigers and cows will be with each other and sheep will move with the wolves.

Isa will stay there for the period of time that has already been decided by Allah. Most believe it to be forty years. Then he will die and Muslims will bury him.

Seeking Knowledge

The Prophet gave great importance to learning. He once said, 'He who goes out in search of knowledge is in Allah's path until he returns.'

Isaiah's Advice

Isaiah was an early prophet. He told people about the coming of Isa and Muhammad. Isaiah used to get revelations from Allah frequently and Israelites used to regard his word with respect and care. The king too regarded Isaiah with great honour. One day, the king got to know of an impending attack by Sennacherib, in whose army was the famous Nebuchadnezzar.

Allah told Isaiah to tell the king that his time was almost up and he should appoint an heir apparent. Hearing this, the king fell down to prostrate and thank Allah for all His bounties, and seek forgiveness for his sins. His prayer pleased Allah who told Isaiah to tell the king that his prayer had been granted, and he would live for a further fifteen years. As for Sennacherib, he need not fear them. As it turned out, Allah sent death upon the invading army, leaving only five of the men alive. They were captured and paraded around the city. Isaiah rose in honour among his people for saving their king and all of them from a deadly fate.

A Cruel Ruler

Sometimes people wonder, 'Why do we have such a cruel ruler? He does not do justice. He kills the innocent, attacks women, the infirm and the old.' The answer was provided by Allah Himself. He sent Jeremiah as a prophet to the people of Israel at a time when they were indulging in sins. Jeremiah preached Allah's message to them. But they did not change their evil practices.

One day, Allah revealed about these people to Jeremiah, 'They do not fear My punishment. Go, and tell them that Allah has spared you till now only because of the piety of your fathers. But you have forgotten My Teachings. I will send upon you a tyrant and cruel ruler who will have no mercy, and will destroy you.'

Soon, Nebuchadnezzar attacked them, killing one-third of the local people and taking as slaves another one-third, leaving only the old and the ailing.

Reviving the Ruins

Uzair was a pious man. Through his prayer he could cure the sick. One day, he was returning from his estate in peak summers. He saw a building in ruins. As it was pretty hot, he decided to rest there for a while. He had with him his donkey and some food. As he looked around, he wondered how Allah would revive the ruins.

He then went to sleep. He went into a deep slumber of possibly, a hundred years. In fact, he was actually dead. Then Allah decided to revive him. He sent an angel to revive his heart and his eyes. After that his bones and flesh were put together.

When Uzair opened his eyes, he was asked by angels for how long had he slept. He replied, 'Maybe a day or a part.' The angels told him he had been dead for a hundred years yet his food and drink had remained fresh due to the grace of Allah. Uzair was thankful to Allah and understood the wisdom of Allah's answer to his question before he had fallen asleep.

Uzair Comes Home

When Uzair was fully revived, he mounted his donkey and decided to go back to his home and neighbourhood. He thought people would recognise him but nobody did, even when he tried to introduce himself. Dejected, he went home. There he found an old lady who was around one hundred twenty years of age, sitting on a stool. She was blind. Uzair asked her, if that was Uzair's home. She replied, yes, and invited him inside. She was delighted to know him as this was the first time after many years that anybody had mentioned that name in the house. Uzair introduced himself, but she did not believe it was him!

So, she found a way to find out the truth. She said, 'Uzair was a pious man whose prayers were always accepted by Allah. Through his prayer he healed the sick. So pray to Allah to return my eyesight. I can then see you and if you are Uzair, I will be able to recognise you.'

Uzair prayed to Allah and then passed his hand over her eyes. Her eyesight was instantly restored! The woman who had been a maid in his home once upon a time, now opened her eyes and recognised Uzair. She was grateful for this miracle. Uzair had returned home.

Reciting the Torah

The maid who had got her eyesight back went to the town to tell everybody that Uzair was alive, and was back and that he had restored her eyesight too. People did not believe her. Among those who doubted her word was Uzair's son. He pointed out that his father had a mole between his shoulders. Uzair uncovered his shoulders and the mole was indeed, there. The son was convinced and rejoiced at his father's homecoming.

The town-dwellers, however, did not believe him. They said that Nebuchadneezar had burnt the Torah. As nobody in their township had memorised it completely the way Uzair had, if he was truly who he claimed to be, he would be able to recite the entire text fluently. Now, the problem was to find a copy of the text so they could prove the challenge they had put forth towards Uzair.

Uzair's son remembered that his father had kept a Torah about which he alone had known. He pointed the townspeople towards that place. The locals went and discovered a copy of the Torah with faded pages and in a fragile condition. Uzair then sat down under a tree, and started reading it. While he read, whatever had gone missing, he rewrote it for everybody's benefit.

Youth and Old Age

When Uzair had gone to sleep in the ruins, he was aged forty. He lay dead for a period of hundred years there. When he was revived by Allah, he was aged forty only. The world had changed yet he remained the same. His eyes, heart, bones and flesh had remained as that of a 40-year-old man.

When Uzair went back to his hometown, he found that the survivors of his youth now looked like old men and women. The maid at his home was twenty when he left. Now, she was a blind woman aged one hundred twenty, and his son was one hundred eighteen! Having slept for a hundred years, it was almost as if time had frozen for Uzair while the world passed by. The son looked much older than the father who though aged one hundred forty, looked like a man in his prime!

Isa's Important Covenant

After Allah revealed the Book to prophets who came before Prophet Muhammad, he took a covenant from them. He said, 'There will come to you a messenger confirming what is with you, you will believe in him, and help him. Will you be bound by this, and take this my covenant as binding on you?' They replied, 'We will be so bound.'

These words prove that Allah took a covenant from every prophet that he will be a believer in all those prophets who will come after him. Thus Adam had to bear witness to the prophethood of all others while Isa, the last prophet before Prophet Muhammad had to take a covenant for only Prophet Muhammad as no prophet came after that. He is the last seal of Prophethood.

Qarun's Arrogance

It is not wealth or children that brings us closer to The Almighty. Rather, it is belief and righteous deeds that take us closer to Allah. Arrogance takes us away from Him. There was a man called Qarun. He had amassed great wealth. It is said that the keys to his treasury were of gold and so heavy those keys could not be lifted by one man. He was proud of his wealth and would spend his days and nights guarding it, losing sleep over it. He would not share even one cent of it with others and did not believe in helping people in times of need and would wonder why he wasn't happy. The locals advised him to avoid being so stingy and to be a little openhearted. It was the grace that Allah had bestowed upon him which he must be grateful for, as it was meant to better the world. If he wanted to be truly happy, he must know that it would only be through good deeds as that would bring him closer to Allah. Allah loves humble, kind-hearted men and women who do good deeds.

Qarun did not listen to them, arguing that all his riches were only his. Allah was displeased with his arrogance. He caused the earth to swallow him and his house. There was no one who could protect him in those few seconds. All his riches were turned to dust and could not be used by him either. It sent a powerful message. It is not material wealth that makes us happy. Rather, it is love, kindness and righteous deeds that take us closer to Allah.

Elias in Damascus

The glorious Quran talks of the Almighty sending His prophets to all nations. Among the prophets and messengers was Elias. He preached about the worship of one God among the people near Damascus in Syria. He said to his people, 'Will you not fear Allah? Do you invoke Bal and forsake the best of creators, Allah, your Lord, and the Lord of your forefathers?'

His people, however, did not believe in him. Bal continued to be a popular idol for them. They attempted to kill Elias for his constant teachings of the worship of only one god. Elias escaped and hid in a cave for many years. When a new king ruled over the area, his luck changed. His teachings remained the same, though. He came out to present to the king the teachings of Islam. Many people became believers. His patience and fortitude prevailed. Allah saved him from the killers because he had faith in Him.

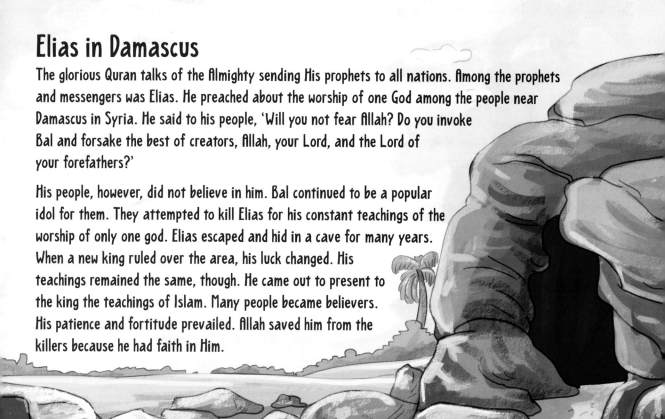

Danyal and the Lions

Danyal was a brave and pious man. He was so brave that he was not even afraid of lions. Once, Nebuchadnezzar captured two lions and threw them into a well. Danyal was brought there and as he believed only in the worship of Allah, he was also thrown into the well so that he would be an easy prey for the lions. The lions though did not attack him. Instead, they lovingly licked him. Danyal stayed with them for a while. He stayed safe.

He was such a pious man that no prayer of his went unanswered. After he had spent some time in the well, he felt hungry. But there was no way of coming out to look for food. So he prayed to Allah. Within no time, Allah sent Jeremiah to him with food and drink. Seeing him at the tip of the well, Danyal was surprised. Jeremiah told him he had been sent by Allah. Danyal was relieved, and said, 'Praise be to Allah, Who does not forget those who remember Him.' Danyal's prayer was similar to the one found in Surah Baqarah of the glorious Quran where Allah says,

'Remember me, I will remember you.'

Danyal Thanks Allah

Danyal was a great believer in Allah. And thanks to the power of his prayer, he came out of the well alive and kicking. Like fire did not burn Ibrahim, lions did not harm Danyal in the well. When he came out of the well, he did not forget to thank Allah. Further, he wanted to remind himself, and the future generations of Allah's generosity, how He had protected him in front of the lions. He decided to get an image done, showing his experience in the well. On that stone Danyal's image was shown along with the two lions licking him. The image talked not of his bravery but Allah's generosity as the lions licked him out of love rather than threatening his life. Danyal used to look at the stone engraving again and again to remind himself of the blessing of Allah upon him.

He realised that no king or animal could harm him as long as he had the support of Allah. His faith was strengthened due to the nerve-shattering experience.

Zakariya's Prayer

Zakariya was an old carpenter. He had little strength left in his body. His muscles had weakened. His wife was old too. They did not have a child. One night when everybody slept, Zakariya prayed secretly to Allah. He prayed for a son so that he would have an heir for his family. He had no fear of anybody watching him and opened his heart in front of Allah. He was confident his prayer would not go unanswered. He said, 'And in calling You my Lord, I have never been unblessed.'

Zakariya had been looking after Maryam who had no apparent source of income, yet was never short of food by Allah's grace. He knew that if Allah could provide her with food and shelter in all seasons, He could provide him a child despite his old age. Allah granted his prayer.

Initially, he had wondered how that was possible as he was old and his wife had never had a baby. Zakariya, therefore, asked for a sign. He was told, 'Your sign is that you will not speak to the people for three nights though you will be in good health.' As Zakariya fulfilled Allah's order, and kept quiet for three nights, he was granted his boon. Thus Yahya was born.

Yahya Endowed with Wisdom

Yahya was a boy ahead of his times. In his years of innocence, he was given wisdom by Allah. He was given the qualities of tenderness and piety. He was kind towards all whom he interacted with. He was an obedient son too.

As a little boy, when Yahya was invited by other children to join them in play, he would turn down the invitation. He knew he had a higher purpose in life. Yahya grew up to be a prophet and spent his life spreading the word of Allah. So much so, that the Prophet said, 'Hasan and Husain are the leaders of youths in the Jannah, except for the two cousins, Yahya and Isa.' It simply meant that Yahya, along with Isa, will be a leader in his own right in Paradise.

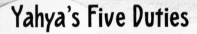

Yahya's Five Duties

Yahya was a devout Muslim. He was commanded me to do five things and ask others to do the same. He carried out his duties, but was worried that if he were to ask others to do the same, he would be punished. One day, he mustered up courage and gathered people in a masjid.

He began by praising Allah, and said, 'Allah has commanded me five things personally and that I should ask you to carry them too. First, you should not worship other than Allah. Never associate anybody with Allah. I command you to pray. Do not let yourselves be distracted in prayer. I command you to fast. The smell of the mouth of a fasting person is purer to Allah than the fragrance of musk. I command you to give charity. I also command you to remember Allah frequently. It makes one feel safe and contented almost like when a man finds refuge in a fortified castle when he is being chased by his opponent.'

Yousha Ibn Noon's Justice

Yousha ibn Noon ruled over Israelites for more than twenty-five years. He was known for being just. Once he went for a battle. He asked his people to accompany him. The ones excused were those who had just got married, a man who had built a house but no roof over it yet and a man who had bought a pregnant goat or camel, and was waiting for their babies. As he went to battle, he entered the town around the time of Asr prayers. He offered his prayer, and soon conquered the town. All the warriors gathered for a share of the spoils.

The spoils were given to the fire. The fire though, did not consume them. Yousha ibn Noon was intrigued. He asked one person from each tribe to come forward and pledge to him. One by one, they came, but one person's hand got stuck with Yousha ibn Noon's. He understood that the man was a cheat. He asked others from that tribe to take the test. The hands of three men got stuck. Yousha ibn Noon declared them to be cheaters. He spotted the ones who had taken the spoils without permssion, calling them cheaters too and declared, 'The spoils of war were not allowed for anyone before us. This is because Allah saw our weakness and incapacity, so He purified it for us.'

Gratefulness in Adversity

Ayub was Lut's grandson. He received the revelation from Allah. He was an extremely rich man in his time. He owned vast tracts of land, cattle, sheep and servants. Then he fell on hard times. He contracted smallpox. No part of his body was left unaffected by the disease. He was expelled from the town for fear of the disease spreading to others. His wife was the only one who stood by him and took care of him. She nursed him, cleaned him and helped him with his needs. As time passed, all of Ayub's riches were spent on food and medicine. She, a woman who was used to an aristrocratic way of life, did not think twice and started working to feed herself and her husband. Ayub's condition worsened. His flesh started disappearing from his body. Only bones and muscles remained. His wife would bring ashes for him, and smear it on his body to cure him and soothe his pain. Ayub bore it all patiently and never complained. He said, 'I had lived for seventy years in a healthy state and I can bear this patiently for Allah for another seventy years.' Such was Ayub's faith.

After some time, people stopped employing Ayub's wife worried that they might contract disease too. She had a beautiful curtain of hair which she would tie in two thick braids. When things became really bad, she was forced to sell one of her braids for food. She did not complain. The next day, the same thing happened. She found no job and had to sell her other braid. By now, Ayub was curious and insisted on knowing the source of her income.

She smiled at him and silently removed her scarf to show him what she had done. That is when Ayub remembered to be grateful for his good fortune and prayed to Allah, 'Harm has inflicted me and You are the most merciful.' Hearing Ayub's grateful prayer in such adverse conditions, Allah took mercy and in an instant Ayub was cured and restored to health!

Ayub's Brothers

When Ayub suffered from smallpox, once his brothers visited him. But they stood at a distance as the stench was too difficult for them to bear. They thought Ayub was suffering due to his own ill deeds and Allah was unhappy with him. One of the brothers said, 'Were Allah to know any good in Ayub, He would not have put him to this trial.' Ayub was hurt and angry. He prayed to Allah, 'O Allah! If You have known that I never spent a night satiated if I had known of a person who was hungry, then prove me true.' A voice answered, confirming his statement. The brothers heard it too. Then Ayub prayed, 'O Allah! You have known that I never had two shirts while I knew of a place where people had no clothes. Then prove me true.' Yet again, a voice came from heaven, confirming what he said. The brothers heard it as well. Finally, Ayub fell down in prostration, pleading for release from suffering. His prayer was granted. Indeed, Ayub was a man who cared for the poor. He would not go to sleep if he knew anybody was hungry. He did not keep any extra clothes with him if he knew people around did not have clothes to cover themselves. Allah answered his prayer when his brothers doubted his integrity and character.

Healing Bath

When Ayub prayed for health, Allah asked him to strike the earth with his foot. He did as ordered. From the spot he struck, Allah caused a spring of cold water to gush forth. Ayub washed himself from that spring. He also drank from it. With that healing bath, Allah removed his disease, taking away his pain and all its marks from his body. As he was having his bath, Allah rained on him golden locusts. Ayub happily collected locusts in his clothes. When asked by Allah, if he was not feeling satisfied, he said, 'O Lord! Who will feel satisfied from Your Mercy?' He was so thrilled with Allah's infinite mercy that he wanted more and more of it after suffering for a long time. It was almost like a man eating after a long time.

A Hundred Better Days

When Ayub was relieved of his problem, his life changed beyond recognition. His wife was away when he recovered his health. When she came back, she was surprised to find a man clad in a dress from paradise. She could not recognise him. She wondered where her husband was. Had the wolves eaten the sick man? She was worried about him and his disappearance. Ayub reassured her and told her he was indeed, her husband. 'Allah has returned my healthy body to me,' he said. It didn't stop there. Allah also returned his wealth and children. He blessed him with more. Ayub, the most patient of men, was richly rewarded for keeping his faith and bearing adversity with dignity and calmness.

Throwing Waste Away

Prophet Muhammad was known to be a man of calm demeanor. His detractors vouched for his integrity. He won over many enemies with his patience and good humour. There was an old woman though who refused to believe in the message of the Prophet. She devised a plan to upset him. She went to the roof of her house and collected all the garbage of her home in a basket. She wanted to throw it at the Prophet who used to pass by her house everyday. The woman was confident he would get angry and she would be able to make a scene of it. That day when the Prophet passed by, she threw all the garbage she had collected from home, at him. He did not react. The Prophet cleaned himself and walked on.

The old woman did the same the next day. The Prophet's countenence remained unchanged. Thinking that the Prophet was too cowardly to act, she made it her practice to throw garbage every day. The Prophet did not react even once.

One day, the old woman fell ill. That day, as the Prophet passed by, he noticed she was not around to throw garbage and became concerned. He went to her door and knocked steadily. She thought he had come to settle scores when she was ill. It was only when she was convinced that he didn't want to quarrel with her that she opened the door. The Prophet asked about her well-being taking care of her with medicine. Over a period of time, he would monitor her state of health and it became a routine for him to visit her every day, asking after her and cleaning her house while making her comfortable.

Seeing the graciously calm and large-hearted nature of the Prophet, the old woman's heart melted in a few days. She felt ashamed at her behaviour and went to the Prophet to ask for forgiveness. As time passed by, she became one of his strongest believers. Thus, through patience and a compassionate heart, the Prophet was able to bring about a positive change where others would have failed!

Faith

An old woman struggled to lift her luggage as she walked down the road. The Prophet saw her and offered to help. He lifted one of her heavy bags and gave her support. He was polite and courteous. Along the way, the old woman started chatting with him. He asked her about her journey. She replied that she was leaving the town due to a man who was leading people astray. He was not good to the people and she did not want to be in such an environment.

The Prophet asked her the man's name. She replied, 'Muhammad.' As they reached the end of the town, the old woman thanked him and asked him his name. The Prophet replied politely, 'I am the same man because of whom you are leaving the town. I am Muhammad bin Abdullah.'

The woman was shocked to hear this! She realised that people had presented a wrong picture in front of her. Impressed with the character of the Prophet, she embraced Islam.

Gratitude

A poor man loved the Prophet and wanted to please him. One day, he brought a bunch of grapes to the Prophet while he sat with his companions. The Prophet ate a grape, then another and yet, another. The companions looked on. Then he finished the entire bunch all by himself. The poor man was very happy to see the Prophet eating all the grapes.

After he left, one of the companions curiously asked the Prophet, on why he had not shared the grapes with the others in company and chosen to eat all the grapes himself. The Prophet replied that the grapes were sour. If any of his companions would have had them, their reaction would have told the poor man that the grapes he had brought were not good.

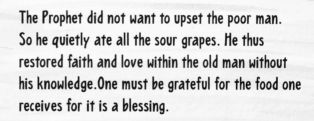

The Prophet did not want to upset the poor man. So he quietly ate all the sour grapes. He thus restored faith and love within the old man without his knowledge. One must be grateful for the food one receives for it is a blessing.

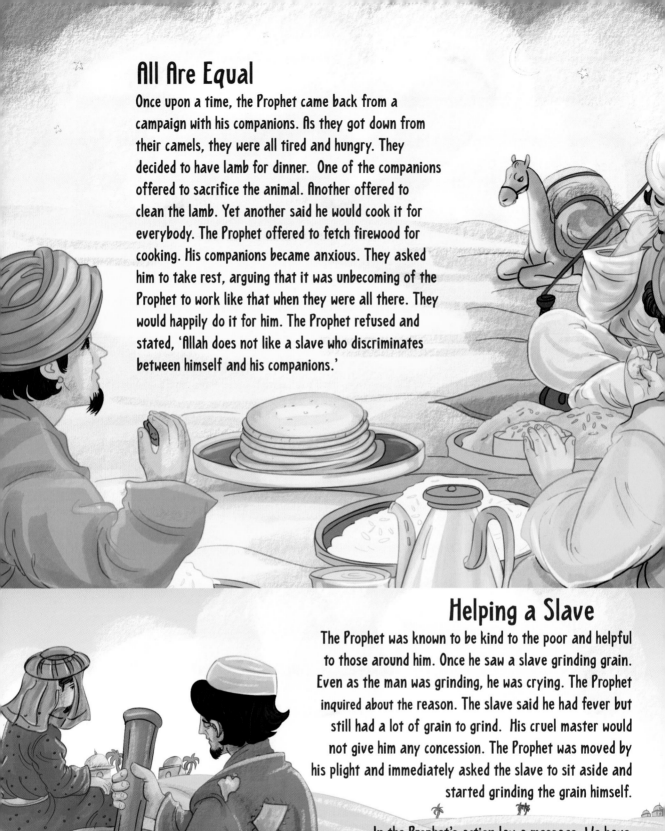

All Are Equal

Once upon a time, the Prophet came back from a campaign with his companions. As they got down from their camels, they were all tired and hungry. They decided to have lamb for dinner. One of the companions offered to sacrifice the animal. Another offered to clean the lamb. Yet another said he would cook it for everybody. The Prophet offered to fetch firewood for cooking. His companions became anxious. They asked him to take rest, arguing that it was unbecoming of the Prophet to work like that when they were all there. They would happily do it for him. The Prophet refused and stated, 'Allah does not like a slave who discriminates between himself and his companions.'

Helping a Slave

The Prophet was known to be kind to the poor and helpful to those around him. Once he saw a slave grinding grain. Even as the man was grinding, he was crying. The Prophet inquired about the reason. The slave said he had fever but still had a lot of grain to grind. His cruel master would not give him any concession. The Prophet was moved by his plight and immediately asked the slave to sit aside and started grinding the grain himself.

In the Prophet's action lay a message. We have to be kind to the poor and share the workload of those overburdened.

Prophet's Word

Once, the Prophet wanted to buy a camel. He came across a man selling one. The Prophet liked the camel a lot and agreed to pay the price the man asked for it. Unfortunately, he did not have the money with him at that moment. So he requested the seller to come with him to his house so he could pay. The man agreed. As they were walking towards the Prophet's house, a passerby saw the camel and liked it. He asked the man its price. The man agreed to sell it to him at a higher price than he would have got from the Prophet. The Prophet protested saying he had already bought the camel. The seller went back on his word and claimed he never sold it to him. The Prophet asked a few of his companions to verify as proof. They refused saying they were not present when the deal was struck. On seeing the commotion, one of the companions who was passing by, stopped. On being told the entire story, he spoke in favour of the Prophet. The Prophet told him that he was not present on the spot when the deal was made so he could not possibly speak in his favour.

The man replied, 'O Prophet, when you said there is no god but Allah we believed you. When you talked of the angels, the Day of Judgment, heaven and hell, we believed you, confident that as Allah's Messenger you could not lie. In comparison, this is such a petty matter.' The Prophet stood his ground.

The Calf

A man needed to travel but he had no camel to ride on. He came to the Prophet to request him to provide a camel for conveyance. The Prophet, however, said he could only provide a calf. The man was surprised and wondered how would he ride a calf? The Prophet smiled and replied,

'Every camel is the calf of a camel.' He meant that every camel, however mature, is still a baby to his parents. The man understood the wisdom of the Prophet's words and was happy to ride the calf.

Youth

The Prophet had a wonderful sense of humour and it was always based on the facts based on his supreme faith. For instance, once an old woman came to him to request him to pray for her so she could enter Jannah. The Prophet replied, 'No old lady will enter heaven.' Hearing this, the pious old woman started crying and asked him why no old woman could enter Paradise.

The Prophet smiled and reminded her of what is written in the Quran. It says, 'Women of heaven will be of young age.'

It was his way of telling the old woman that after being raised again on the Day of Judgment, people will once again be young when they reach Jannah. Such wit and lightheartedness remains unmatched to this day and is testimony to the wonderful character and personality the Prophet possessed.

Do it Yourself

It was a long and exhausting summer. The caravan of the Prophet and his companions halted in search of water. Every man got down from his camel and went in search of water to perform ablutions in preparation for prayer. The Prophet got down too. But he did not sit and wait. Suddenly, the Prophet went back to his camel, tied its knees and started looking for water. The companions were surprised to see the Prophet walk back to the camel for such a small thing and said they would have happily done it for him if he had told any one of them.

However, the Prophet was not one to trouble others for his needs. He replied to his companions, 'Never seek others' help in your affairs, don't lean on others, even if it is a small piece of Miswak (the wood used for brushing teeth).'
The Prophet championed the do-it-yourself mantra.

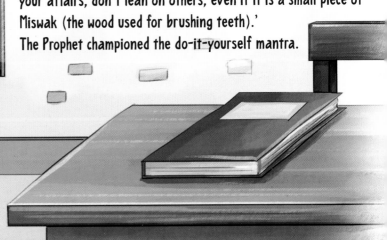

Races with His Wife

The Prophet was blessed with a sporting nature. He did not mind having an impromptu match with his wife Ayesha. Once the Prophet and Ayesha were travelling with the caravan when the Prophet asked the caravan to move ahead while he would follow with his wife. After the companions had moved a fair way, he challenged his wife to a race. Ayesha, then quite thin, defeated the Prophet in the race. He was not to mention this race in conversation again.

Time lapsed. Once again, there came a time when the Prophet was travelling with his wife in a caravan. After a while, he requested the caravan to move ahead while the couple stayed behind. As the caravan moved ahead, he once again challenged Ayesha to a race. By then, Ayesha had gained a few pounds. She was, however, sporting enough to race. This time the Prophet defeated her. After the victory, he said, 'Now, we are even.' The joy and purity of spirit, just like that of a child, was a mesmerising scene for his wife to behold.

Angel's Wing

The residents of Sodom used to harass the travellers. They would often rob them. They were greedy and immoral men and women who lacked character and respect for life and people. No matter what Prophet Lut told them about living a decent life, they paid no heed to his advice. When the men got to know that the Prophet had handsome guests, they immediately proceeded to his house. They were keen to see the guests and take them with them. Prophet Lut shut the door and wished to set them right for insulting his guests.

As they threatened to smash the door open, one of the guests, actually an angel, stepped out. He spread out his wing, hitting many men with it. The men touched by the wing were blinded and went back groping. The guests stayed safe.

Differences

Islam insists on equality of human beings. In a gathering, people are expected to sit wherever they find space, irrespective of their educational or economic status. Once it so happened, that the companions of the Prophet were sitting with him. A poor man entered, and finding space, sat next to a wealthy man. The rich man drew his clothes closer and shuffled ever so slightly. The Prophet noticed that he was trying to avoid physical contact with the poor man. He said,'Are you afraid that some of his poverty might touch you? Or are you afraid that some of your riches might fly off to him?'The rich man answered in the negative initially, before understanding the implications of his actions. This realisation, as he sat before the Prophet, made him see a new perspective.He promised half of his wealth to the poor man in atonement. At this, the poor man rose in protest and declined the offer, saying, 'If I take his offer, some day I might be as arrogant towards the poor.' In the Quran, therefore, arrogance is considered a sin.

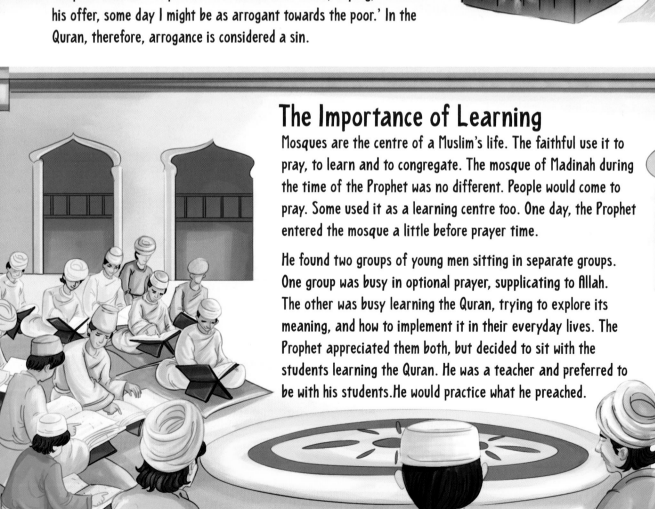

The Importance of Learning

Mosques are the centre of a Muslim's life. The faithful use it to pray, to learn and to congregate. The mosque of Madinah during the time of the Prophet was no different. People would come to pray. Some used it as a learning centre too. One day, the Prophet entered the mosque a little before prayer time.

He found two groups of young men sitting in separate groups. One group was busy in optional prayer, supplicating to Allah. The other was busy learning the Quran, trying to explore its meaning, and how to implement it in their everyday lives. The Prophet appreciated them both, but decided to sit with the students learning the Quran. He was a teacher and preferred to be with his students.He would practice what he preached.

Mercy of the Prophet

Taif is a city about forty miles from (the city of) Makkah. But until the Prophet left Makkah for Taif, nobody in Taif followed Islam nor was anybody aware of Islam. When the Prophet reached Taif and introduced himself with the purpose of spreading Islam, the local people mocked him. They used to worship idols. Hardly anybody believed in him. One of the local men taunted the Prophet, saying, 'I must be naive or a thief if I believed you to be a prophet.'

The locals even set up a group of children to chase him away. The children threw stones at him. The Prophet started bleeding badly. Tired and bleeding from head to foot, the Prophet decided to take some rest in a garden that belonged to two rich men, Atabah and Shaibah of the Quraish tribe. The Prophet belonged to one of the clans of the same tribe. They noticed the Prophet sitting alone, and the Prophet sat there and prayed, 'O Allah! I seek refuge in Your light which illuminates darkness and straightens the affairs of this world and hereafter, that Your displeasure and wrath may not descend upon me. For the sake of Your pleasure, I remain pleased and resigned to my fate. No change in this world occurs without Your Will.'

On hearing the Prophet pray, an angel offered to help him. 'O Prophet of Allah! If you order us then we will grind the people of Taif between mountains.' But the Prophet refused to let them kill the locals. He said, 'I am sent as the prophet of mercy, not to punish people.'

Adaas Comes Around

As the Prophet sat all by himself in the garden, he was hungry and tired. The garden belonged to two rich men, Atabah and Shaibah of the Quraish tribe. The Prophet belonged to one of the clans of the same tribe. They noticed the Prophet sitting alone. Adaas brought him some grapes. As the Prophet was about to start eating, he invoked the name of Allah. Adaas had never heard something like that in Arab society. He was impressed by the recitation.

The two exchanged introductions and the Prophet said, 'I am the Prophet sent by Allah. Adaas replied, 'I am Adaas, a Christian from Nainava.'

The Prophet was happy to hear the mention of Nainava. He said, 'You come from a place where my brother Yunus lived.' Now it was Adaas who was pleasantly surprised. He asked, 'What do you know of Yunus? Here no one seems to know him.'

The Prophet explained, 'Yes, I know him because just like me, he was a prophet of God.' Adaas was moved by the Prophet's persona and thoughts. His very aura made Adaas go down on his knees before the Prophet. Kissing his hand, he embraced Islam.

Serving the Prophet

A companion of the Prophet, Mohammed Anas was well versed with the Prophet's eating habits. He knew his favourite food as well as the time for ingesting a specific food item. He knew the Prophet liked to break his fast with some dates and milk. So he would prepare accordingly. Similarly, the Prophet used to have some light food at suhoor time before he commenced his fast.

One day, as the sun set, Anas waited with iftar for the Prophet. It was dark but the Prophet did not reach for iftar. So Anas ate the food himself and prepared to retire for the day. Just then, the Prophet reached with another companion. Anas had no food left. He looked around but found no food at home. He felt awkward and the blood rushed up to his cheeks in embarassment . The Prophet understood his plight . He did not say a word and went to sleep hungry that night. Such was the wisdom and kindness of the Prophet that he never breathed about this incident to anyone!

Living in Harmony with Nature

Islam lays great stress on planting trees. Planting a tree is regarded to be an act of great piety, one which continues to pay dividends even after death. One gets rewarded for any wayfarer who might take shelter under the tree, which was once planted or a bird, which might eat from it.

Once Prophet Muhammad is reported to have said, 'If the Hour (the day of Resurrection) is about to be established and one of you was holding a palm shoot, let him take advantage to plant it before the Hour is established.' In another Hadith, he is reported to have said, 'If a Muslim plants a tree or sows seeds, and a bird or a person or an animal eats from it, it is regarded as a sadqah(charity) for him.'

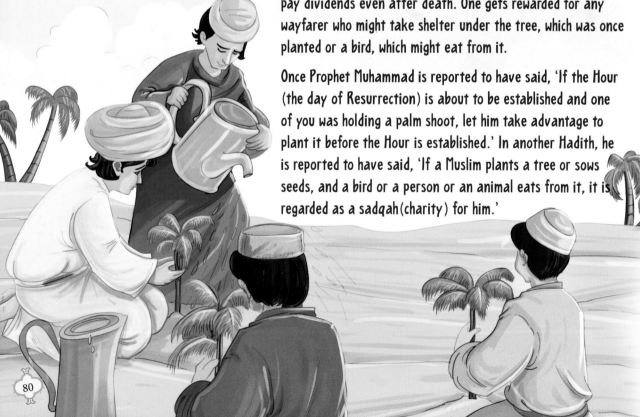

Conserve Water

Children tend to play with water when they go to have their daily bath in the summers. One finds adults as well, letting the tap run when they wash their face, brush their teeth or even perform ablution for prayer. In the Prophet's time he would have chided them for it. It is said that the Prophet saw a man performing his ablutions for prayer while using water very liberally. The Prophet asked, 'Why this wastage?'

The companion replied, 'Is there wastage in wudu too?' He probably believed that since he was getting ready for prayer it did not amount to wastage. The Prophet said, 'Yes, even if you are at a flowing river.' The Prophet was against the wastage of water even in areas where water existed in plenty.

Keeping the Environment Clean

The Prophet laid great stress on keeping the environment clean. He used to help with household work at home, stitch and repair his clothes and help with the churning of wheat. That is why, even sweeping and dusting our home is part of our duty in Islam. The Prophet believed that even removing a piece of stone from the path of the people amounted to charity.

Interestingly, though during the time of the Prophet, there were no flush toilets, he asked his companions to beware of three things: relieving themselves in a shaded place, i.e. places used by people; relieving themselves in walkways or near a watering place. All this was done to keep not just the houses clean from inside but also to keep clean the immediate outside environment, and by extension, the whole town too.

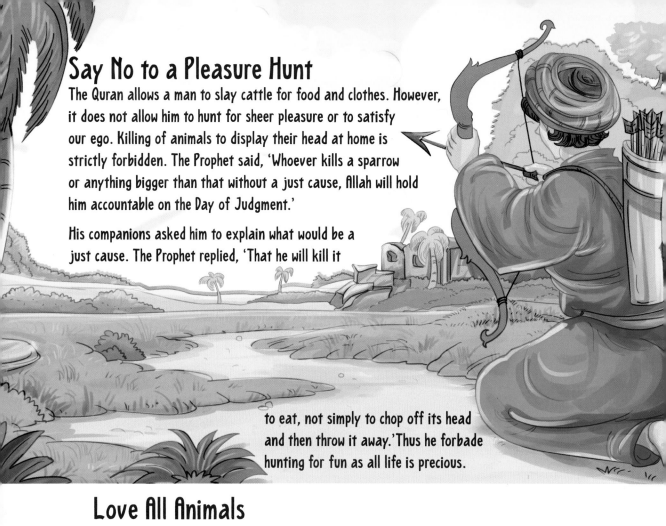

Say No to a Pleasure Hunt

The Quran allows a man to slay cattle for food and clothes. However, it does not allow him to hunt for sheer pleasure or to satisfy our ego. Killing of animals to display their head at home is strictly forbidden. The Prophet said, 'Whoever kills a sparrow or anything bigger than that without a just cause, Allah will hold him accountable on the Day of Judgment.'

His companions asked him to explain what would be a just cause. The Prophet replied, 'That he will kill it to eat, not simply to chop off its head and then throw it away.' Thus he forbade hunting for fun as all life is precious.

Love All Animals

It was peak summer. A man was walking all by himself, in the scorching heat of the desert. He was very thirsty. Not finding a drop of water anywhere, he was happy to spot a well. He went down and quenched his thirst. At last, he felt relieved and rejuvenated.

As he came away after quenching his thirst, he saw a dog panting. The dog's tongue hung out. The dog was licking the wet mud to quench his thirst. The man understood that the dog was very thirsty. Once again, he went to the well. This time, he took off his shoe and filled it with the water from the well. He then held the shoe in front of the dog so that he could drink water from it. The dog happily drank the water.

For this one deed, the sins of the man were forgiven. Allah appreciated his action. As the Prophet said, 'There is a reward for serving any living being.'

Of Depraved Souls

A man who believes in Allah, establishes prayer, and gives in charity, goes to heaven. On the other hand, a man who does not believe in Allah or His Messenger, does not pray, and spreads corruption on earth, goes to hell. Anybody who has sinned, no matter how seriously and how often, has the doors of pardon open till death arrives at his doorstep. Then his repentance is of no value.

Allah says in the Quran, 'If you could see when the wrongdoers taste the pangs of death and the angels stretch their hands out, (saying), 'Deliver up your souls. This day you will be awarded a degrading punishment.'

That degrading punishment starts immediately after his last breath. When he is about to depart from the world, angels with black faces descend from the heavens. They carry with them rough haircloth, and sit around the person about to die. Then the Angel of Death sits at the head of the unbeliever and says: 'O foul soul, come out to the wrath and anger of Allah!' Then the Angel of Death violently pulls the soul out of the body, leaving the person in unspeakable pain. But as soon as the Angel of Death takes the soul, other angels sitting around the person get into action. They wrap the soul in the rough haircloth. A foul smell is emitted from the cloth. As they move away with the soul, other angels ask them, 'Who is this depraved soul?' They introduce the person with the most hated names, relating the soul to the living parents and relatives. The doors of heaven at this point remain closed. It is then reunited with the body. The trial would begin in the grave itself. As soon as the mourners of the departed person move forty steps from the grave, the trial begins.

Do unto Your Brother

Do unto others what you would have them do unto you. The Prophet always advised the believers to choose for their brother, what they would choose for themselves. If they bought a particular shirt for themselves, they were expected to a buy a similar shirt of around the same price for gifting. It was never proper to eat the best and dress up in the best clothes yourself, while gifting inferior items to others .

So particular was the Prophet about not making a difference between oneself and one's brother, that he said, 'He who supplicates for his brother behind his back (in his absence), the angel commissioned (for carrying dua to his Lord) says:

'Ameen, and it is for you also'.' So next time you pray for your brother, be sure that an angel is praying the same for you.

Talk Well or Keep Quiet

The Quran asks us not to gossip and not to entertain any judgements about people. We are asked not to call anybody by ugly nicknames or to run down others. It may be they are better than us and we are not aware of it. If some loose talk or gossip session is on while we are sitting at a place, we are advised to move away from the group. Similarly, it tells us to cross-check any news that we come across. Else we may regret it later if the news proves to be false. It might also spoil our relationship with people if we do not take this safeguard. It advises us to be quiet instead of backbiting for

a person who indulges in backbiting is like a man who eats his dead brother's flesh.

Prophet Muhammad said, 'Whoever believes in Allah and the Last Day should talk what is good or keep quiet.'

Pray for Paradise

The Prophet wanted us to be regular with our prayers. The Quran talks of establishing prayer rather than merely praying. Establishing prayer means to pray in a group or congregation in a proper manner. The Prophet asked the faithful to do good deeds, and do them sincerely. He said to his companions, 'The deeds of anyone of you will not save you (from the Hell fire),' he said, adding, 'Even I (will not be saved) unless and until Allah bestows His Mercy on me. Therefore, do good deeds properly, sincerely and moderately; and worship Allah before noon and in the afternoon and during a part of the night; and always adopt a middle, moderate, regular course whereby you will reach your target (Paradise).'

Importance of Prayer

When Prophet Muhammad went on miraj (ascension) Surah Bani Israil was revealed to him. By the time Surah Bani Israil was revealed, he had been teaching monotheism to people for close to twelve years. During this time, the followers of the Prophet grew marginally and the opponents left no stone unturned to obstruct the growth of his faith. The verses of Bani Israil spell out to the Arabs the manifesto of Islam. The surahs (verses) provide guidelines according to which the Prophet could direct the lives of the faithful. These guidelines became invaluable later when the first Islamic state was built in Medina.

Interestingly, this was the first occasion when the five daily prayers were declared obligatory and their time was clearly laid down.

Beginning of the Hijri Era

Since the first revelation, life became more challenging for the Prophet and his companions. After about a decade of preaching, he had to send some of his followers to Ethiopia for their safety. Those who remained back in Makkah faced great persecution. The Prophet, therefore, had to send seventy of his followers to Medina, which was then called Yathrib. A few years later, he learned of a plot to kill him alongside Abu Bakr. So he too set off for Medina.

It was not easy. The enemies of Islam set off in pursuit of the Prophet and his companion. The two of them took refuge in a cave. A spider spun a web at the opening of the cave. The attackers from Makkah saw the unbroken web and mistook the cave to be desolate. They went away. The Prophet and his companion reached Medina safely. A spider's web had saved their life.

This migration of the Prophet from Makkah to Medina, known as hijrat, was to be the beginning of the Islamic calendar.

Support in Madinah

Prophet Muhammad was aware of Medina and the way of working of the locals. In fact, before he migrated to Medina, envoys had gone to Makkah asking Prophet Muhammad to come and mediate a dispute between two tribes. Such was the Prophet's reputation for justice that nobody doubted that he could favour one against the other. Once he reached there, the Prophet found a lot of popular support and the local tribes forgot their personal rivalry for some time to rally around him. He was soon to have Ansars or helpers as also Muhajirun or emigrants who had migrated with him from Makkah. Together, they all moved against the pagans of Makkah. Soon the Battle of Badr started. The Muslim army was outnumbered one to every three people but they succeeded against their enemies.

Battle of Uhud

The people of Makkah had lost the Battle of Badr but they believed the war still remained. So, the forces of the town were united again. An army of three thousand men was gathered. They attacked the Muslims at Uhud, which was a ridge on the outskirts of Medina. This time, they succeeded. The Muslims were driven back to Medina. The Prophet too was wounded.

The Makkans knew that the Medina army would strike back. As predicted, two years later, the Makkahn army came back with a much greater force of around ten thousand men. The army attacked Medina. This time, at the famous Battle of the Confederates, the Muslims prevailed because of their sound defense. The Muslims had dug up deep trenches which made the Makkahn cavalry movement impossible. The Makkans retreated. And Medina stayed safe for the Muslims. This was an important turning point and there is a surah named after the confederates in the Quran.

First Constitution

As peace prevailed in Medina, Muslims set about building a federation and framing the rules of life. It was around this time that the Prophet assumed complete leadership of the confederation and sent letters to kings ruling over different empires at that time. He sent letters to the king of Persia, king of Ethiopia, the governor of Egypt and the emperor of Byzantium. He asked all of them to embrace Islam.

At the same time, the tribes in Medina accepted him as the Prophet of Allah. With him at the head, they formed a confederation. Interestingly, there was a place for people of other religions in Medina. The Jews were considered part of the community, and were taken as protected people as long as they conformed to local laws. Same was the case with Christians who too were allowed to stay in Medina and enjoy religious freedom as long as they paid their taxes. However, those who worshipped more than one god were not allowed entry into Medina.

Faith of the Prophet

Prophet Muhammad and his companions made great sacrifices to establish Islam. They were subjected to physical and economic pressure, persecution and starvation. But they did not leave Islam.

Companions like Bilal, the first man to pronounce athaan, Umm Ubays and Ammar ibn Yasir had to go without food and water for days together. They were beaten mercilessly, made to lie on scorching sands and boulders were placed across their chest so that they groaned in pain. But they did not move away from Islam. Professionals were not given their wages after work was completed, if they continued to worship Allah and regard Muhammad as His Prophet. The persecution was almost unbearable.

One day, a companion went to meet the Prophet who was resting near the Kaaba and said, 'O Messenger of Allah! The oppression has now reached its limit. Would you not pray to Allah?' Hearing this, the Prophet turned red, and reminded him of the sacrifices of earlier generations for the cause of faith. He said, 'Believers before you were subjected to greater oppression. Yet they did not abandon their faith. Believe me, Allah will accomplish this mission.' If faith can shake mountains, his faith would change the destiny of many generations.

Migration to Ethiopia

For five years after the revelation came to Prophet Muhammad, people who embraced Islam had to bear taunts and ridicule, economic boycott and physical violence. One day, the companions of the Prophet, eleven men and four women, decided to migrate to Ethiopia. They had heard great things about the ruler Negus, who was known to be a man of justice. The Prophet too, advised them to stay there till Allah found a way out for them.

All fifteen went together but the enemies, the Quraish, got to know of their plan and chased them. However, they were able to get on a boat to Abyssinia and thus avoided being killed by the Quraish. After some time, they were joined by more Muslims, making it eighty-three men and eleven women on the way to the kingdom of Negus.

The Quraish, however, did not rest. They sent valuable gifts to Negus and his courtiers with an emissary and requested him to send the migrants back. Negus decided against sending the migrants, arguing that he could not let down people who had escaped from their towns to his kingdom for safety.

He decided to investigate the matter, and called the migrants to send their leader to him. Negus asked them why they had fled. One of the companions, Jafar, explained to him the teachings of Prophet Muhammad and recited the opening verses of Surah Maryam. The verses dealt with Prophets Yahya and Isa. Negus heard them with rapt attention and tears trickled down his face. He returned the gifts of the Quraish, and allowed the migrants to stay in Ethiopia also called Abyssinia.

Umar Embraces Islam

Umar was an angry man, known for his tendency to be violent. One day, he set out to kill Muhammad. Along the way, he met a man who advised him to first set his own house in order, before trying to kill the Prophet. He was hinting at Umar's sister Fatimah, and her husband Said.

Hearing this, Umar rushed to Fatimah's house. As he reached there, he found her and Said reading from a scroll. She tried to hide the scroll from him. Umar hit her husband. As she tried to protect her husband, he hit her too on the head. She started bleeding but refused to give up the scroll. Moved by the sight of his bleeding sister, Umar asked her again to show him the scroll. She agreed, provided he pledged that he won't tear it. Umar agreed. Then Fatimah asked him to wash himself before touching the scroll. He did, as asked. And started reading from the scroll. On it was written Surah Taha of the Quran. As he read it, he exclaimed, 'What a remarkable discourse!' He was probably referring to the story of Musa that the surah talks about. Finishing the surah, he went out to meet the Prophet, and became one of the faithful companions of the Prophet. Islam grew in leaps and bounds through Umar.

The Fall of Makkah

The popularity of Prophet Muhammad grew fast in Medina. He was able to make harmonious alliances among various warring tribes. His early years had been spent with the Bedouin and stood him in good stead in his understanding of dealing with people. The number of his followers also, therefore, increased significantly. Confident in his teachings, and support of his companions, the Prophet demanded access to the Kaaba from the Makkans. This action by itself denoted great success, for a little earlier, the Prophet had to migrate from Makkah to Medina to save his life and that of his followers. Now, he was able to negotiate on an even footing with the dwellers of his city of birth.

A year later, in 629 AD, the Prophet conquered Makkah. There was no bloodshed.

Invitation to All

The Quran makes it the responsibility of every Muslim to invite everybody to Islam. A small part of Surah Qasas, verse eighty-seven says, 'Invite them to your Lord'. This invitation to Islam or opening the portals of faith to all, started after the fourth year of the Prophethood of Muhammad.

The first addressees were the Quraish, who, over the next few years were to leave no stone unturned in adding to the hardship, of the believers. The Quraish had managed Hajj and Umrah pilgrimages since the times of Ibrahim and even managed to install the popular idols of various tribes inside the Kaaba. So when Prophet Muhammad preached against polytheism, it gave rise to opposition. The Prophet started his invitation exercise in a low-key, wise manner. He organised a feast to which he first invited his close relatives. Around 45 people, members of the Banu Hashim and Banu al Muttalib clans attended the feast. His uncle Abu Lahab, however, spoiled the feast with his words and all the guests left.

The Prophet organised another feast a few days later. This time, he spoke to them about the essential tenets of Islam. He told the guests that they were to be held accountable for their deeds. This time, Abu Talib supported him, though he did not abandon his age-old religion.

Meanwhile, the Quraish leaders did not oppose the Prophet at the beginning. But when he preached against idolatry, they found in him a threat to their religion, and became openly hostile. They were concerned that the Islamic principle of all being equal before Allah would rob them of their traditional superiority. To counter this, a verse of Surah Hujurat was revealed to Prophet Muhammad which said that superiority among human beings was based on reverence to the Creator and compassion to His creation.

Going Grey

Once, Abu Bakr was talking to the Prophet. He observed, 'I see you ageing. What is the cause of it?' The Prophet agreed with him and revealed, 'The surahs Hud and its sisters have turned my hair grey.' In other words, the Prophet was going through a tough time when Surah Hud was revealed.

He was torn between two issues. On one side, the Quraish tribe was relentless in its hostility to Prophet Muhammad. On the other, he was being revealed verses of the Quran through which Allah sent stern warnings of severe punishment to those who did not respond. The Prophet was worried that the time given to people to mend their ways might end any day. The Prophet therefore, went grey, worrying about the people.

The Prophet's Pardon

When the Muslims were undergoing severe persecution, Allah sent Surah Yusuf to the Prophet. In these verses, the story of Prophet Yusuf and his brothers is recalled. However, as one listens to the story, one realises that it was also applicable to the Quraish tribe at that time. In the famed story of Prophet Yusuf, his brothers connived to get rid of him, but finally had to fall at his feet and seek pardon. Similarly, Prophet Muhammad and his followers were assured that all the troubles created by Quraish will vanish. A little under two years after these verses were revealed, the Quraish hatched a conspiracy against the Prophet. And like Prophet Yusuf, Prophet Muhammad too was forced to migrate. Again, like Prophet Yusuf, Prophet Muhammad too gained ascendancy in exile. Like Prophet Yusuf pardoned his brothers for their evil designs, Prophet Muhammad too, pardoned the Quraish tribe. When the Quraish sought his pardon, the Prophet replied, 'I say to you what Yusuf said to his brothers, 'No blame lies with you today. May Allah forgive you. He is the most Merciful of all those who are merciful. You may go, all of you are free.'

Speaking Courteously

The companions of the Prophet gave him utmost respect. Occasionally though, they would get into an argument among themselves in his presence. They would even raise their voice with him. Allah did not like that they should speak in such a manner or in a loud voice in the presence of the Prophet. So Allah revealed, 'O You who believe! Raise not your voices above the voice of the Prophet, nor speak aloud to him as you speak aloud to one another. Lest your deeds be rendered fruitless while you perceive not.'

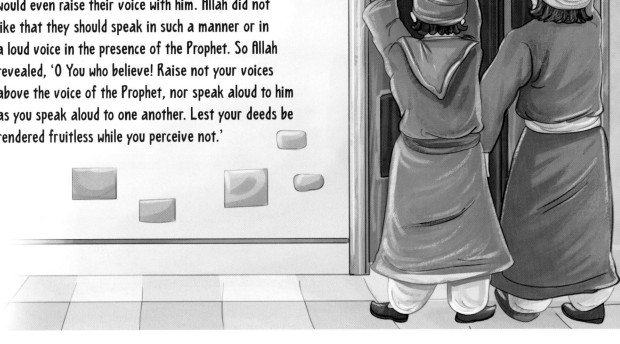

Defaming People

Ridiculing others never pays off. We all have our strengths as well as our weaknesses. We may be better than others in one respect and others are better than us in another respect. The Quran tells us not to make fun of others. Ridiculing others hurts them and shows a degree of arrogance and a fake illusion of superiority. Calling names, body shaming and bullying people is not the way of a Muslim.

No Backbiting

It is easiest to talk of somebody who is not present. It is equally easy to eavesdrop on somebody's conversation. We must avoid both. We are told through the Quran's Surah Hujurat, not to spy nor to indulge in backbiting. A person who backbites is compared to a man who eats the flesh of his dead brother. Surely, something none of us would like to do.

Deeds Define Mankind

The Quran has a very interesting take on the world we live in. Surah Hujurat says, 'O mankind, indeed We have created you from male and female and made you peoples and tribes that you may know one another. Indeed, the most noble of you in the sight of Allah is the most righteous of you.' This world with its oceans and mountains, rivers and plains, people, dark and fair; was created to give man a chance to blossom in different circumstances. Geographical divisions were made to identify people, not to divide them. Allah created nations, races and communities to celebrate their uniqueness and not to exclude them. It is only through our noble deeds that we can become great. Nothing else will help define us.

Brothers All

At some time or the other, we all fight with each other. Yet we all need Allah's mercy, as all of us sin too, at one time or another. How does one find a way out? The Quran gives it through Surah Hujarat, which tells us we are all brothers. And when brothers fight, it is better to help them make peace. Says verse ten, 'The believers are but brothers, so make settlement between your brothers. And fear Allah that you may receive mercy.'

Remembering the Lord

At the slightest sign of a problem, we often go back to our parents. We consult friends too. They are our support system which Allah created. It is in our interest to take help from Allah directly, as He always loves and remembers us every second of our lives. We are told this through the longest surah of the Quran, Surah Baqarah. Verse one fifty two tells us, 'So remember Me; I will remember you. And be grateful to Me and do not deny Me.' Anytime of the day or night you can reach out to Him and He will always be there as your twenty-four by seven hotline!

Be and it Is!

We are told by our teachers in school to be brave and to keep our chin up even when we lose. Positive thinkers tell players not to look at the strength of the opponent, but at their own strength to win the match. The Quran tells us the very same thing. We must be positive and believe in ourselves, and Allah, as he is the best of strategists. Our opponents plot and strategise. They conspire and manipulate. But remember, the best of strategists is Allah. And when you are with Allah, nobody can hurt you and nobody can defeat you. For anything to be done, He just has to say 'Be', and it is. Kun, fayakun.

Endless Humiliation

There are people who hurt us, who injure us, who say bad words to us. But they never seem to get caught. Next time these thoughts cross your mind, tell yourself that Allah does not take us to account immediately. He does not punish us immediately for any wrong deed. Rather, He gives us a chance to make amends. And for those who continue to make mistakes, He gives them a long leash. Almost like a dog on a very long leash. The dog thinks he is free. So he runs about, but when the leash is pulled back, he is kept close and disciplined. Similarly, wrongdoers are not left scot-free. They are given a chance by Allah to make their wrongs right, after which they are taught their lessons as He is the just One.

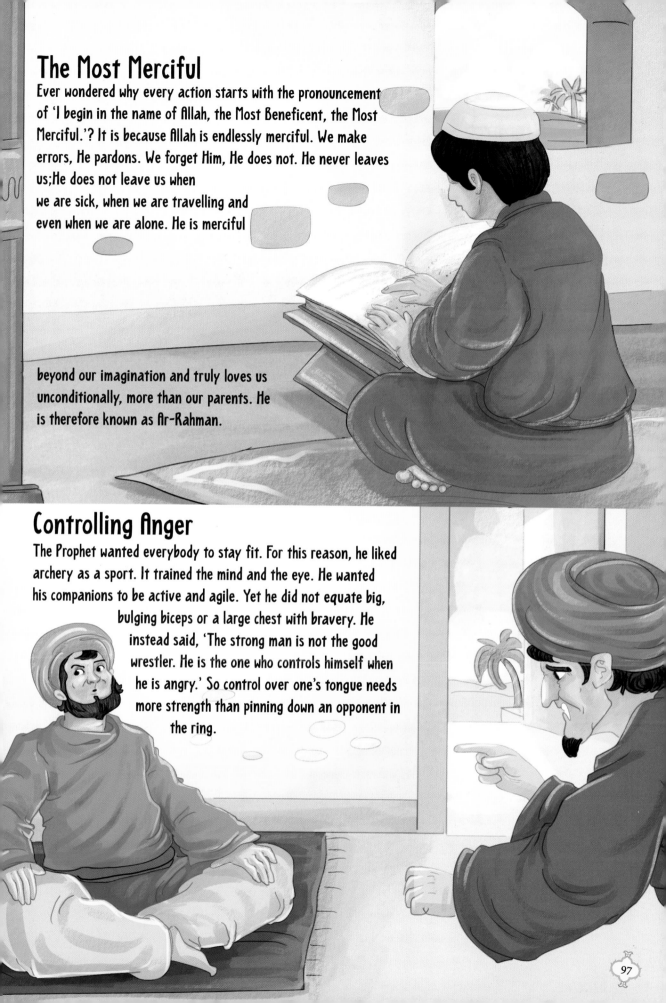

The Most Merciful

Ever wondered why every action starts with the pronouncement of 'I begin in the name of Allah, the Most Beneficent, the Most Merciful.'? It is because Allah is endlessly merciful. We make errors, He pardons. We forget Him, He does not. He never leaves us; He does not leave us when we are sick, when we are travelling and even when we are alone. He is merciful

beyond our imagination and truly loves us unconditionally, more than our parents. He is therefore known as Ar-Rahman.

Controlling Anger

The Prophet wanted everybody to stay fit. For this reason, he liked archery as a sport. It trained the mind and the eye. He wanted his companions to be active and agile. Yet he did not equate big, bulging biceps or a large chest with bravery. He instead said, 'The strong man is not the good wrestler. He is the one who controls himself when he is angry.' So control over one's tongue needs more strength than pinning down an opponent in the ring.

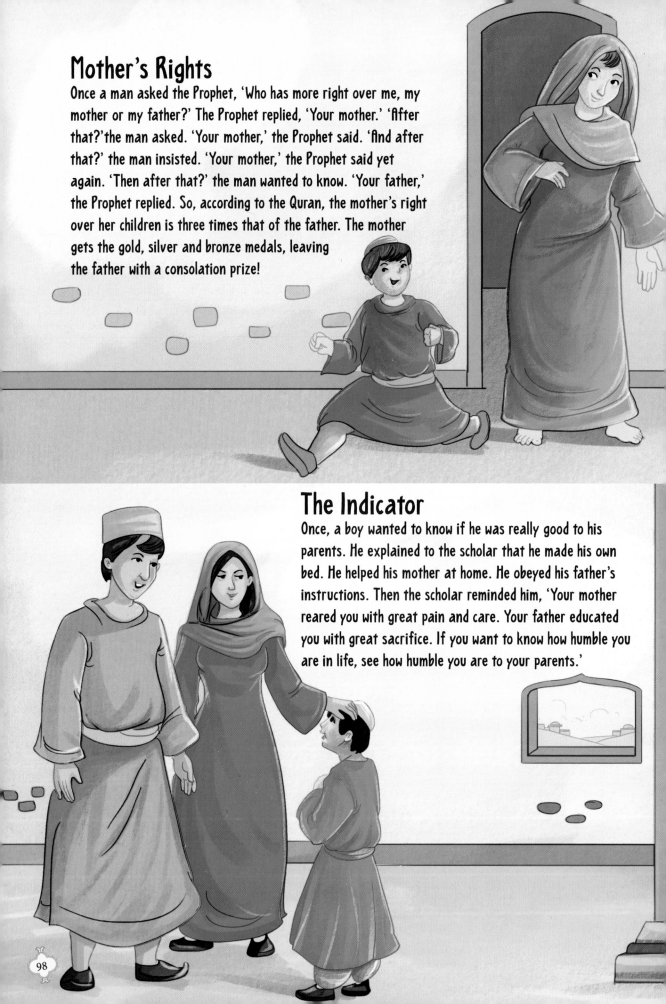

Mother's Rights

Once a man asked the Prophet, 'Who has more right over me, my mother or my father?' The Prophet replied, 'Your mother.' 'After that?' the man asked. 'Your mother,' the Prophet said. 'And after that?' the man insisted. 'Your mother,' the Prophet said yet again. 'Then after that?' the man wanted to know. 'Your father,' the Prophet replied. So, according to the Quran, the mother's right over her children is three times that of the father. The mother gets the gold, silver and bronze medals, leaving the father with a consolation prize!

The Indicator

Once, a boy wanted to know if he was really good to his parents. He explained to the scholar that he made his own bed. He helped his mother at home. He obeyed his father's instructions. Then the scholar reminded him, 'Your mother reared you with great pain and care. Your father educated you with great sacrifice. If you want to know how humble you are in life, see how humble you are to your parents.'

Looking Outside

A man had done a lot of charity in his life, prayed regularly and lived in the company of good people. As his end came, he did not gain Paradise. Many were surprised. Then Allah explained that the man had done all this to gain glory in the world, so people would give him name and fame for his good deeds. He had already reaped the fruit of his efforts in this world as he wished. The Hereafter worked differently and needed one to focus with their inner spirit and conscience rather than the world outside.

Importance of Prayer at Night

A girl came to an alim (a learned scholar), crying. She wanted her mother to be healthy again. Her mother had been sick for long. The girl's prayers were not being answered. The alim told her, 'Give yourself a few minutes before Fajr.' The girl did not understand. He explained, 'Get up a little before Fajr (the early morning prayer), offer two rakah (cycles) of salaat (prayer facing Makkah) and ask Allah whatever you want. It will be granted. That prayer never goes in vain as the night is a testimony of what a person loves the most: Sleep or anything over and above it. Therefore the prayers would be the purest. Allah would never deny prayers offered with purity of heart.

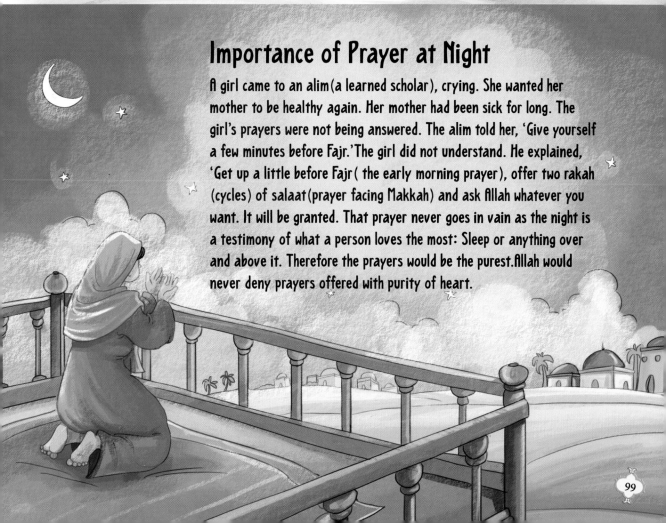

No Distractions

During the time of the Prophet, it so happened that once a caravan of traders landed just when the Khutbah (public preaching)for Friday prayers was about to commence. Many men started taking great interest in the merchandise on sale. Some started striking a bargain. Allah did not like this. He commanded through Surah Jumuah of the Quran, 'And when they see some merchandise or some amusement, they disperse headlong to it, and leave you (Muhammad) standing (while delivering the Friday Khutbah). Say,that which Allah has is better than any amusement or merchandise! And Allah is the best of providers.'And so it happened as men were asked to move for Friday prayers, leaving everything aside.

Cross-check Things

It is important not to believe every piece of information that comes our way through social media or the television. One must cross-check facts with an unbiased mind.The Surah Hujurat, verse six of the holy Quran tells us to cross-check news, lest we regret later. We must always hear both sides of an argument before arriving at a decision, so that we do not regret it later. So if a friend comes to us with a complaint about another friend, it is important to hear the other friend too. He will have his story to relate.

Share Information, not Rumours

When we get information that may affect public safety or well being, it is critical not to spread any rumour. Instead, we are supposed to bring it to the notice of the authorities concerned. That way, the public will not do any thing in panic, and the information can be accessed, and cross-checked for any remedial action. The Quran brings to light this dictat beautifully. It says, 'When there comes to them some matter touching (public) safety or fear, they make it known (among the people)... Instead, it would have been better for them if only they had referred it to the Messenger or to those charged with authority among them, the proper investigators would have understood it from them directly.'

The Three Plaintiffs

Once a companion of the Prophet, Abu Hurairah, was asked to relate a Hadith that he had heard from the Prophet. He recalled, 'When the Day of Judgment comes, Allah will come down to judge the people. And every nation will be kneeling in submission. The first people to be called forth will be a man who had learned the Quran by heart, a man who was killed for the sake of Allah, and a man who had a lot of wealth. Allah will say to the reciter (of the Quran), 'Did I not teach you that which I had revealed to My Messenger?' He will say, 'Of course, My Lord!' Allah will say, 'What did you do with what you were taught?' He will say, 'I stayed up at night and during the day (to recite it).' Allah will say, 'You have lied. You only wanted it to be said that so and so is a reader, and it was said.' The one who had a lot of wealth will be brought forward. Allah will say to him, 'Did I not give generously to you so that you will not be in need of anyone?' He will say, 'Of course, Lord.' Allah will say, 'What did you do with what I gave you?' He will say, 'I used to give it to my relatives and in charity.' Allah will say, 'You have lied. You only wanted it to be said, so and so is generous, and it was said.' Then the one who was killed for the sake of Allah will be brought forward and Allah will say, 'What were you killed for?' He will say, 'I was commanded to fight in jehad for your sake so I fought until I was killed.' Allah will say, 'You have lied. You only wanted it to be said that so and so was courageous. And it was said.' Then the Messenger of Allah struck my knees and said, 'O Abu Hurairah, these three are the first people for whom the (Hell) Fire will be heated on the Day of Resurrection.'

Seeking Pardon

We all make mistakes and repent. We repeat our mistakes. We seek pardon again. The Prophet had something to say regarding this behaviour. He said, 'Every son of Adam makes mistakes, and the best of those who make mistakes are those who repent.' Allah gives us a chance to make amends for the mistakes we commit. The best way of dealing with our errors is to make istighfar (seek His pardon) and follow it up with tauba (make a pledge that you won't repeat the sin). So, a naughty boy gets a chance to atone for his mischief by seeking Allah's pardon.

Praying in One Garment

Once a gentleman prayed wearing only a cloth tied around the middle at the back. A devotee saw him and asked, 'Why are you praying in only one garment?' The gentleman asked him in turn, 'Who among us had two garments at the time of the Prophet?' With this statement, he proved that it is permissible to pray in only a lower garment, though, of course, it is better that one does so in two. His one sentence set at rest all the doubts of common people and intellectuals alike about the clothes to be used for prayer.

Solar Eclipse

It is said that day Prophet Muhammad's son, Ibrahim passed away, there was a solar eclipse. Many people attributed the eclipse to the death of the Prophet's son. The Prophet corrected them, saying, 'The sun and the moon are the signs of Allah. They do not eclipse due to the death of anyone. If you see them eclipsed, then pray to Allah until the eclipse is over.' With this anecdote, the Prophet tried to tell his followers that what was a natural occurrence could not be implied to have any religious or symbolic value.

Following Wrong Ways

The Prophet and his companions were going from Makkah when they came across a lotus tree. The tree was held sacred by the mushrikeen (those who joined others in worship of Allah) and they used to hang their weapons on that tree. Seeing the tree, the companions asked him to make for them a similar tree. Indeed, they wanted their own version of the lotus tree.

It reminded them of the deeds of the people of Musa who took to worshipping the calf in his absence. Some of the people at that time had wanted to have a deity of their own. The Prophet replied, 'By the One in whose hand is my soul, you have said what the people of Musa said to him. It is the same thing, and you will follow the ways of the people who came before you, step by step.' History would repeat itself if one were not careful.

Civility in Language

We belong to Allah, and to Him we shall return. Once upon a time, Ibn Umar and Umar ibn al-Khattab were discussing something. Ibn Umar found Umar ibn al-Khattab swearing by his father. This seemed ungracious. The Prophet called them over, and told them that Allah had forbidden them to swear by their forefathers. Anyone who wanted to swear could swear by Allah's name or stay silent. This prevents uncivil behaviour and helps people recentre themselves towards peace.

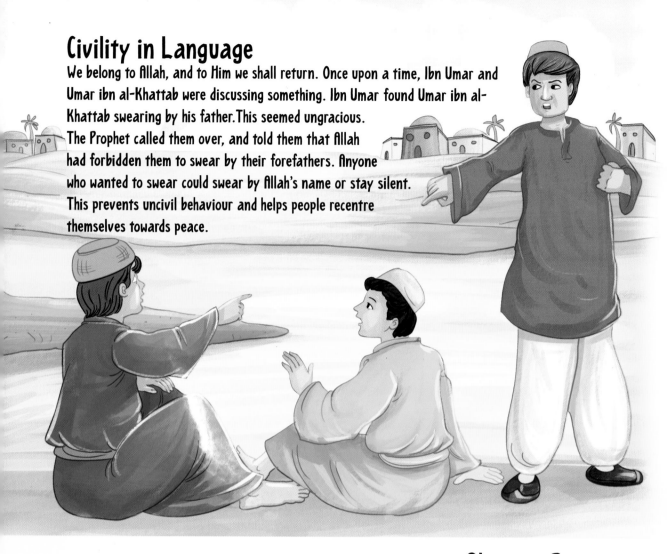

Sleeping Positions

A poor man came down to stay with the Prophet. The Prophet was happy to host him and looked after his well-being personally. At night, he would check on his guest to ensure that he was comfortable. One night, the Prophet found the guest sleeping on his chest. The Prophet pulled him off him and said, 'Allah hates this. Don't lie like this.' For physiological reasons, it is appreciated that one sleeps on the right side or straight on the back and never on the chest and stomach. Sleeping on the left side can put stress on your internal organs that need rest at the end of the day .

Greater Jehad

Jehad stands for struggle. It is a struggle to control internally the impulse of our own desires, our own passion. Jehad can be of two types: lesser Jehad or war against others; and the greater Jehad, that is constant fight against evil within. Once, the Prophet and his companions had come back from war. The companions were happy and beginning to settle in peaceful times, when the Prophet remarked that they had left lesser Jehad for greater Jehad. All knew that was a bigger challenge, though a worthier one.

Simplicity

The Prophet always emphasised simple living. Though sent as a prophet to the entire humanity, he lived a completely simple life. No angels heralded his arrival, no courtiers walked behind him. He wore no gold bracelets and necklaces. He wore no silk or velvet. He even did his work himself. At home, he used to help out with domestic responsibilities and often repaired his clothes and shoes himself. There were times, when for days on end he did not have anything to eat. Yet he never complained. Such was the man who is remembered by the world nearly one thousand four hundred years after he passed away.

Taking Care of Parents

Once upon a time, the Prophet was preparing for war. His companions too were busy putting together their weapons. Just then, a man approached the Prophet. He too wanted to join the war. He considered it his call for Jehad.

The Prophet asked him if his parents were alive. The man replied in the affirmative. The Prophet then asked if they were old. The man again nodded his head in agreement. The Prophet then advised him to go and serve his parents as service of aged parents was more reward-worthy than setting out for war against an enemy.

Passing By

It is forbidden to pass in front of somebody who is offering prayers. Once the son of Marwaan came in front of Saeed al-Khudri while he was praying. He stopped the child. When he did not stop, he hit him. At this, the child went back to his father to complain. The father asked al-Khudri the reason for treating the child in such a manner. The man told him that he had heard the Prophet say that if anybody is praying and somebody had to pass through the same place, let him wait as much as he can. But the child was not prepared to wait.

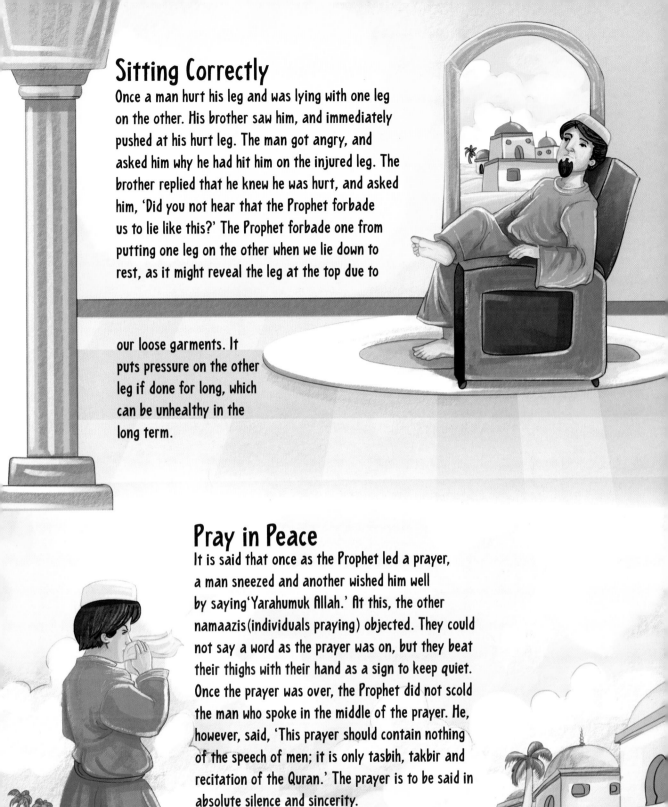

Sitting Correctly

Once a man hurt his leg and was lying with one leg on the other. His brother saw him, and immediately pushed at his hurt leg. The man got angry, and asked him why he had hit him on the injured leg. The brother replied that he knew he was hurt, and asked him, 'Did you not hear that the Prophet forbade us to lie like this?' The Prophet forbade one from putting one leg on the other when we lie down to rest, as it might reveal the leg at the top due to our loose garments. It puts pressure on the other leg if done for long, which can be unhealthy in the long term.

Pray in Peace

It is said that once as the Prophet led a prayer, a man sneezed and another wished him well by saying 'Yarahumuk Allah.' At this, the other namaazis (individuals praying) objected. They could not say a word as the prayer was on, but they beat their thighs with their hand as a sign to keep quiet. Once the prayer was over, the Prophet did not scold the man who spoke in the middle of the prayer. He, however, said, 'This prayer should contain nothing of the speech of men; it is only tasbih, takbir and recitation of the Quran.' The prayer is to be said in absolute silence and sincerity.

Prayers after Eating

The Prophet ate his meal. Having done the ablution earlier, he got up to pray. At this, a companion brought him water to do the ablution again. The Prophet rebuked him and continued his prayers. The companion was hurt, not sure if he had upset the Prophet or done anything wrong. After the prayer, the Prophet said, 'He brought water for me to do wudu after I had eaten something. If I had done wudu (ablution) then all (companions) would have done the same. They would have thought they had to do wudu every time they ate something.' The Prophet was a role model for all his companions. If the companions saw him doing a thing, they thought it was necessary for them to do as well. The Prophet, having performed ablution once, did not want to repeat the cycle for fear of setting in motion a different practice.

Effort and Intention

The Prophet, in one of his sermons, revealed, 'If a ruler judges and strives to make the right decision, and his decision is correct, he gets two rewards. If his decision is wrong, he will still have one reward.' In Islam you are judged by your effort, your intention, not by the results.

For instance, if a person tries to do what is fair but still does not succeed, he cannot be held guilty of lack of effort. On the other hand, if a man does not care about making a mistake, he is held responsible. This rule applies to all, irrespective of status, gender or creed. All you are asked to do is to make an effort with a good intention.

The Judge

The Prophet was very keen on ensuring that people were fair. According to the Prophet, judges are of three types. The best one is the judge who knows the truth and decides according to it. He will be welcomed to Paradise. Then comes the judge who knows the truth but does not act according to it. He will not gain entry into Paradise. The third type is the one who neither knows the truth nor makes an effort to know it, yet judges. That man will not enter Paradise.

Kill Ignorance

The cure of one who does not know, is to inquire, said the Prophet. Rather than to not know, it is better to ask for complete information. It so happened, that a man during the time of the Prophet, was hit by a stone on the head when he was in an impure state. He went off to sleep. When he woke up, he asked the men around, if he needed to take a bath or he could do with tayammum or ceremonial cleaning. The men told him, he needed to take a bath to clean himself. He had a bath and passed away. When the Prophet came to know what he had been told, he said, 'They have killed him. Why did they not ask if they did not know.' The man had developed fever because of the injury. And bathing in that condition added to his suffering. Ignorance had taken its toll.

Adil

Allah is Adil, the one who does and loves justice. In the Quran, He reminds us again and again to be fair in our dealings. He loves the ones who stand up for what is fair and just. This insistence for fairness can be seen in verse 152 of Surah Ana'm, 'Whenever you give your word (judge between men) say the truth.' Similarly, verse 90 of Surah Nahl tells us, 'Indeed, Allah orders justice and good conduct and giving to relatives and forbids immorality and bad conduct and oppression. He admonishes you that perhaps you will be reminded.' Allah tells us to speak the truth even if it goes against ourselves or our people who are dear to us.

Judge by Action, not Person

A woman borrowed some jewellery. She went to the market and sold it, keeping the money with herself and not informing the owner of the jewellery. The matter was brought before Prophet Muhammad. Usamah, the son of the Prophet's much loved Zayd, spoke in favour of the woman. At this, the Prophet's face turned red, and he said, 'Are you interceding concerning one of the punishments prescribed by Allah?' Usamah sought his forgiveness. In the evening, the Prophet said, 'The people who came before you were destroyed because if one of their nobles stole, they would let him go.

Five Tenets of Islam

Once Prophet Muhammad was asked about Islam, its basic principles and its pillars. He replied, 'Islam is based on five principles. First is to testify that none had the right to be worshipped but Allah. Prophet Muhammad is His Messenger.

To offer salaat, the compulsory congregational prayers five times a day, pay zakaat (i.e. obligatory charity), perform Hajj pilgrimage to Makkah and observe the fast in the month of Ramadan.' If one observes these five, one becomes a practising Muslim.

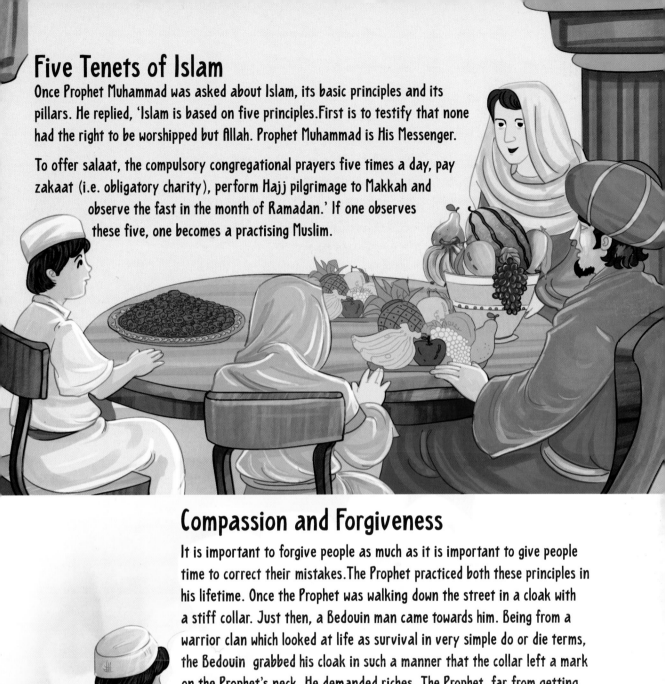

Compassion and Forgiveness

It is important to forgive people as much as it is important to give people time to correct their mistakes. The Prophet practiced both these principles in his lifetime. Once the Prophet was walking down the street in a cloak with a stiff collar. Just then, a Bedouin man came towards him. Being from a warrior clan which looked at life as survival in very simple do or die terms, the Bedouin grabbed his cloak in such a manner that the collar left a mark on the Prophet's neck. He demanded riches. The Prophet, far from getting annoyed at the manner of being approached, calmly asked his companions to give him some wealth as the man needed the money more than them. The Bedouin was surprised at such positive behaviour and asked for forgiveness, deciding to change his rough ways to a more civilized behaviour in the future.

Awareness

The Prophet would always have his companions around him to give him company. Once they went on a pilgrimage together. The Prophet decided to rest at a place called Al-Arj. The companions too followed the Prophet and stopped their journey to take some rest. Aishah, one of the wives of the Prophet, sat near him while the rest of the companions, like Abu Bakr and others, sat around him. After some time, it was time to continue. Abu Bakr was waiting for his camel to arrive. It was supposed to be brought by a slave who arrived but the camel was nowhere to be seen. It was a hot day and Abu Bakr unusually lost his cool, and started hitting the slave mercilessly as that was the only camel he had for the journey ahead. The Prophet saw this and said, 'Look at what this muhrim is doing.' Muhrim is a person who has tied the ihram (pilgrimage dress) to his body. In such a condition, a man is not allowed to cause harm to any bird, insect or animal. The Prophet's wise comment brought Abu Bakr back from his fit of anger and he felt ashamed of his behaviour. The Prophet did not intervene forcefully because Abu Bakr was not known to make such mistakes often. Thus, the Prophet found a quiet way of pointing out his errant action.

Charity

Prophet Muhammad was never hard on youngsters. He would correct their mistakes in a gentle way so that they were never embarrassed. Once, Al-Hasan ibn Ali was with him. He took a date from the bunch that had been given in charity and started eating. The Prophet noticed it. He, however, corrected him in a gentle manner, saying, 'Don't you know we do not eat anything given in charity?' Charity must be used where it is intended to be used and where it is needed.

Permission to Enter

Children are supposed to take permission before they enter their parents' bedroom. If they want to approach their mother at night or during the afternoon siesta, they must first call for her and not just rush in. The Quran guides us to do the same. Incidentally, once the Prophet was having a bath. Just then, his little daughter Zaynab came running in. The Prophet did not scream at her. Instead, he playfully took a fistful of water and threw it at her, saying, 'Go away, foolish girl!'

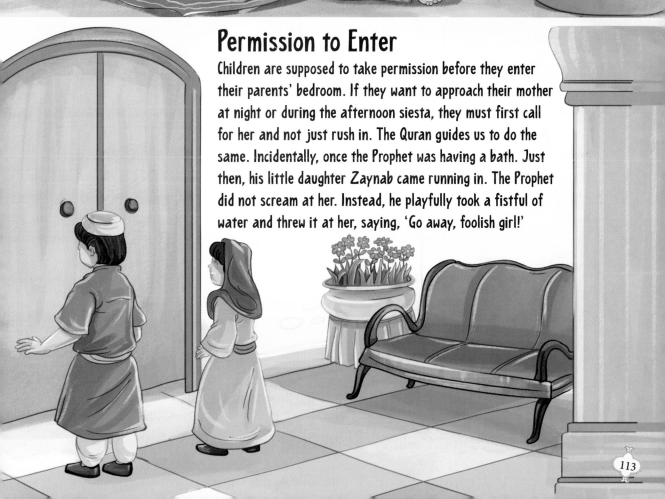

Observing Rituals

It is said that the Prophet corrected a little boy who was eating in front of him. The boy was laying his hand wherever he wished on his plate. The Prophet corrected him, 'Say Bismillah at the beginning of your meal. Eat with the right hand. And eat from what is directly in front of you on your plate.'

It is said in many Hadiths that we should eat with the right hand. When we enter a masjid, we must enter with the right foot. When we leave the masjid, we must leave with the left foot first. The rules are reversed for the restroom. When you enter the restroom, do so with the left foot. When you leave after attending to the body's needs, the right foot should be the first one out of the restroomt.

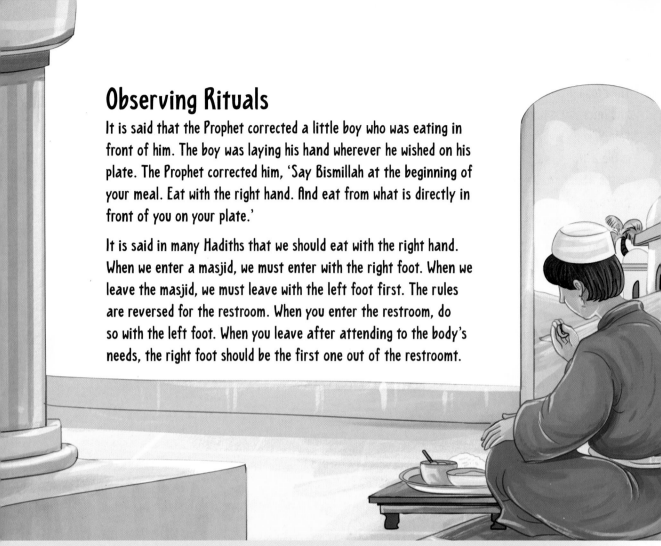

Help

A person who is a victim of somebody's cruelty, needs help. What is important to understand is that the man who inflicts cruelty or does something wrong, needs help too. The Prophet believed that the man who suffered from cruelty needed relief from atrocities but the man who inflicted it needed help as well, as he did not realise the wrong he was inflicting on himself for the Hereafter. Both deserved help equally. He revealed, 'Let a man help his brother whether he is a wrongdoer or the victim of wrongdoing. If he is a wrongdoer, he should stop him. If he is the victim of wrongdoing, he should come to his aid.'

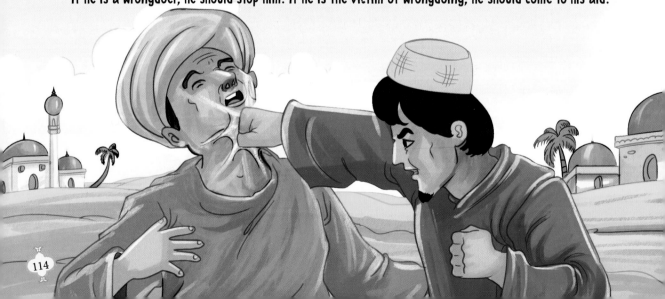

The Prophet's Advice

The Prophet came to rescue humanity. He warned against wrong deeds and informed people about the rewards for their good deeds. He once said, 'My example and the example of people is that of a man who made a fire. When the fire was lit, whatever was around it, including moths and other insects started falling into it. The man tried his best to prevent them from falling into the fire. But he was overpowered, and they rushed into the fire. Similarly, I take hold of the knots at your waist to prevent you from falling into the fire, but you insist on falling into it.' It meant that only those who would listen to the Prophet's advice would be saved from entering the fire in their afterlife.

The Supreme Quality of Kindness

One of the prime qualities of Allah is He is endlessly merciful. He is the best of those who forgive. He loves those who forgive. Even when He permits us to right a wrong, He appreciates it much more if we forgive those who do wrong, who hurt us, who are cruel to us. In an oft-repeated Hadith, Prophet Muhammad is reported to have said, 'Allah will not be merciful to those who are not merciful to mankind.'

The Omnipresent

Allah sees all that we do. He knows what we say and what is hidden in our heart. He knows when we make up things about Him. Prophet Muhammad stated, 'Allah said, the son of Adam tells lies against me though he has no right to do so. And he abuses me, though he has no right to do so. As for his telling lies

against me, he claims that I cannot recreate him as I created him before; and as for his abusing me; it is his statement that I have a son. Glorified I am! I am far from taking a wife or a son.'

Punishing the Evildoers

Among the billions of people who inhabit this earth, everybody's fingerprints are different. These fingerprints will be used to recognise people on the Day of Judgment. There are no escape routes for people. If people believe in Him and do good deeds, they will be rewarded. For those who spread corruption on earth and disbelieve in Allah, they will be punished. They will stay in Hellfire. Yet at the same time, anybody who might have done a tiny good deed, even something as small as that of the size of a mustard seed, will be rewarded.

All Are Equal before Him

When Prophet Muhammad taught the message of Islam in his region, Arab society was divided on the basis of race and tribes. Girl children were often buried alive. There were frequent wars between tribes to establish their supremacy. Might was considered right. When the Prophet preached the equality of all human beings irrespective of their gender, tribe or region, most people were opposed to him. But the Prophet always regarded the nation or tribe to be just an identity for the purpose of recognition. And the only thing that elevated man was his good deeds. As said in the Quran, 'O mankind, We have created you from a single pair of a male and female, and rendered you nations and tribes so that you might know one another. The most honorable of you in the sight of Allah is the one who is most conscious of Him. Allah is All-Knowing, All-Aware.'

The Importance of Peace

Allah loves peace. The first greeting of a Muslim is Assalam-o-alaikum which is nothing but a wish of peace for the person in front. Allah never allows us to fight without a just cause for the benefit of mankind and He does not like war, not even a holy war. What Islam permits is a just war. Even that war has its rules: women and children, the ailing and the aged, all are to be protected. Crops ready for harvest are not to be touched. Through Surah Baqarah of the Quran, we are told, 'And fight in Allah's cause against those who wage war against you, but do not commit aggression – for, verily, Allah does not love aggressors.'

Further, if the opponents offer peace, that offer must be taken up. Allah tells us in the Quran, 'Thus, if they let you be, and do not make war on you and offer you peace, Allah does not allow you to harm them.' The Prophet never picked up arms unless attacked and did not allow others to do so as well.

The Quality of Worship

Once upon a time, some people came to the houses of the wives of the Prophet. They wanted to know his ways of worship. The wives explained it in detail to them. But they found it too little and talked at length about how they worshipped. They thought that for the forgiveness of sins, one needed to perform all the rituals of worship at length to please Allah more. One of them decided, 'From now on, I will pray every night.' Another said, 'I will fast for the rest of my life, and will never break the fast.' The third one said that she would never marry as it may please the Omnipresent better. The Prophet heard them, and said, 'By Allah! I am the one who fears Allah more than anyone. But I fast and I break

my fast. I pray and I rest. And I have been married. Whosoever goes away from my Sunnah, has nothing to do with me.'

Extremist Behaviour

Moderation is preferred in Islam. Extremes were always avoided by the Prophet. Even in matters of worship, he did not permit his followers to leave worldly duties or to punish themselves in the name of devotion. There was a man called Kahmas Al-Hilali who embraced Islam and became one of the companions of the Prophet. He went away for a year. After a year's absence, he came to meet the Prophet. He had become very skinny and the Prophet failed to recognise him. He introduced himself and revealed that he had been fasting for the past year and never once had he slept at night. The Prophet's companion was proud about his devotion. Hearing this, the Prophet said, 'Who told you to torture yourself? Fast in the month of patience (Ramadan), and one day of every month besides that.' When Al-Hilali insisted on doing more as he did not feel adequate contentment, the Prophet allowed him to fast for three days in a month besides the month of Ramadan, but no more than that. Extremes were avoided. Thus, moderation is an integral part of Islam.

Rich or Poor

A man happened to pass by the Prophet who was sitting. He did not recognise him, so he asked a companion about the passerby. The man sitting close by replied, 'This man is the noblest of men. If he were to propose marriage, he deserves to be accepted. If he intercedes, his word deserves to be respected.' The Prophet did not reply. Just then a poor man passed by. Again, the Prophet asked the man sitting close to him about him. The man replied, 'He is a poor man. If he proposes marriage, he should not be considered. If he intercedes, his word should not be heard.' After the poor man had left, the Prophet said, 'This man is better than an earth full of men like the other man.' The Prophet was against discrimination based on material riches as man is known through his actions and spirit.

Interpreting Words

It was narrated by Usaamah ibn Zayd that once, following the instructions of Prophet Muhammad, he went on a military expedition. During the battle, he caught a man. The man said, 'La Ilaaha Ill-Allah.' But Usaamah killed him. Then he felt bad about it, and mentioned the incident to the Prophet. The Prophet questioned him, 'He said, "La ilaaha ill-Allah" and you killed him?' Usaamah replied, 'He only said it because he was afraid of my weapon.' The Prophet asked him, 'How can you know what is in his heart? How can you be sure whether he was sincere or not?' The Prophet kept repeating these words. Only Allah knows what is in a person's heart.

Kindness

Kindness to the poor is highly recommended in Islam. Once, a companion was very upset with his servant. He was beating him. Just then, the Prophet came and called out sternly from a distance. As the companion was very angry, he did not hear the voice of the Prophet until the Prophet stood next to him. On seeing the Prophet, he dropped his whip in fright. Prophet Muhammad reminded him in a

firm voice, 'Allah has more power over you than you have over this slave.' The companion released the slave and pledged never to hit a dependant again.

The Spirit of Cleanliness

Once, a Bedouin man came to a mosque. He was found attending nature's call on the premises. The companions were shocked and asked him to stop. The Prophet saw what the companions were trying to do and asked them not to disturb him. He did not rebuke him or take stern action against him. When the man was through with his business, Prophet Muhammad very kindly explained to him that mosques were supposed to be a prayer house, a place where one remembers Allah and a place to collect for all things good, pure and pious. He was welcome to use it as a sanctuary for prayer and meditation. Then he asked one of the companions to pour a bucket of water over the place where the Bedouin man had attended nature's call and wash the premises thoroughly. The mosque remained pristine.

The Cursed Wind

The Quran tells us to speak only good words or stay silent. We are not allowed to abuse or curse. Once upon a time, a man stood against a gust of wind. The wind was strong enough to blow his cloak away. The man cursed the wind for putting him into an uncomfortable position. The Prophet heard him cursing the wind and disapproved of it. He said, 'Do not curse it for it only

does what it is commanded, and if a person curses something that does not deserve to be cursed, his curse will come back upon him.' What energy you give out to the universe will come back to you the same way one day. So be kind, do good deeds, help others and have good intentions for people around you, for you never know what comes back!

Many Ways, One Direction

There are various ways in which people recite the Quran. During the time of the Prophet, there happened to be a dispute around it. Umar heard a man called Hishaam recite Surah Furqan in prayer. He thought he was doing it differently from what he had been taught by the Prophet. He waited for the prayer to be over. Once the prayer was over, he met Hishaam and told him clearly that his way of recitation of the surah was wrong. He then, took him to the Prophet. The Prophet heard Hishaam first, and said 'This was how it was revealed.' Then he asked Umar to recite. He did as instructed. The Prophet said, 'This is how it was revealed. The Quran was revealed with seven different ways of recitation. So recite in the way that is the easiest for you.'

Circumstances

A companion of the Prophet entered Madinah with his uncles and saw a beautiful garden in the distance. He entered it. As he entered, on closer inspection he saw that it was a wheat field. He took some wheat and started rubbing it. The owner came, and took away his cloak. The companion went to the Prophet to complain and the owner of the garden was called. The owner explained to the Prophet that the companion had taken some of his wheat and rubbed it. In retaliation, he had taken possession of his cloak. The Prophet said, 'You did not teach him if it was a matter of not knowing. And you did not feed him if it was a matter of him being hungry. Give him back his cloak.' The owner was then commanded to give some wheat to the companion. What the Prophet meant was that it is essential to find out the circumstances of a situation before arriving at a decision.

Keeping Close

Prophet Muhammad never imposed a diktat over his companions. It so happened that whenever he stopped to take rest, his companions would spread out around the valleys and mountains. The Prophet did not approve of it. But he confined himself to merely saying, 'Your dispersing in these valleys and mountains is from Shaitaan.' His one sentence was sufficient to stop all in their act. From that day, he never had to ask the companions to stay close together. Legend has it that if a cloak was spread over them, it would cover them all. Such was the respect they had for the Prophet's word and his wisdom.

Harmony

When a man prays in a congregation, he is said to gain twenty-seven times greater reward than if he were to pray alone. The idea is to promote a feeling of fellowship and togetherness. The Quran too asks us to establish prayer, as different from merely offering prayer at home. When men stand up for prayer together in a saff (row), they are asked to stand shoulder to shoulder, ankle to ankle. There is no difference of rich or poor, young or old. All divides evaporate as one stands up for prayer. There is a Hadith which explains it as, 'Straighten your rows (for prayer), or Allah will make you divided.'

Allah Be Praised

We are always expected to follow the middle path, be it in criticism or praise. Just as stinging criticism should be avoided for any minor mistake, lavish praise should be shunned too. It is said that once a companion saw a man and said to the Prophet, 'O Messenger of Allah, there is no one other than the Messenger of Allah who is better than so and so.' Prophet Muhammad disapproved of it straight away. He said, 'Woe to you! You have cut your companion's throat. You have cut your companion's throat.' He repeated the expression several times, then added, 'If any of you insists on praising his brother, let him say, 'I think so and so is such and such, and Allah knows the truth.' He told them he did not affirm anyone's good conduct but rather said, 'I think so and so....' Nobody was given a blanket sweeping approval as in reality only Allah knows the truth.

Letting Praise Go

The best praise is given when the person is absent. Any praise in front of the person can be motivated or exaggerated, to make him feel better than he actually is. The person praised in exaggeration will start believing an illusion and can become arrogant. As a friend, one is bound not to make him feel that way. Pride is never good for a human being. Only Allah has a right over it.

Just as the Prophet advised against lavish praise for these very reasons, he told the person who is praised to seek Allah's forgiveness for any exaggeration people might be guilty of in their high opinion of him. He asked them to say, 'O Allah, forgive me for what they do not know. Do not hold me responsible for what they say, and make me better than what they think.'

The Qiblah

Once Prophet Muhammad saw somebody spit in the direction of the qiblah(direction of prayer). He was deeply upset with this and immediately got down to cleaning the place. He is reported to have later said, 'When any one of you stands up to pray, he is talking to his Lord. His Lord is between him and the qiblah. So, no one should spit in the direction of the qiblah. He should spit to the left or under his feet.'

Pray for Your Brother

Islam forbids jealousy. When we desire something which somebody has, it is best to pray to Allah for ourselves as als well as for our friend. It so happened, during a journey that the Prophet had undertaken with his companions, that the caravan stopped at a place for a breather. One of the companions, Sahl ibn Haneef was said to be a handsome man with glowing skin. One day, as he was taking a bath, he took off his garments. Just then, a companion, Aamir saw him and was left awestruck at the beauty of his body. He exclaimed, 'I have never seen what I have seen today, not even the skin of the virgin.' Hearing this, Sahl collapsed. Prophet Muhammad was told about what had happened. He admonished Aamir and advised him to ask for a blessing for Sahl. 'The evil eye is for real. Do wudoo and help Sahl,' he told him. Aamir did as instructed. Sahl recovered, and continued his journey with the Prophet.

Look Down in Prayer

In prayer, a person may cross his hands at the waist or across the chest. However, his eyes have to be on the ground. Specifically, his eyes have to be at the point of prostrations or sujood. When a person stands in front of the Lord, he is expected to keep his eyes low. He should neither look around or look up towards the sky for he could face plenty of distractions. Prophet Muhammad denounced such an action in no uncertain terms. He said, 'What is the matter with some people who raise their gaze towards the heaven while they are praying? They should stop doing that, or else Allah will take away their sight.' Indeed, once the Prophet was told about a man who kept fiddling with his beard in prayer. The Prophet immediately told him he won't do such a thing if he understood he was standing in front of God.

Concerned Neighbours

Once a man came to the Prophet and complained about his neighbour. The Prophet advised him to put up with the troublesome neighbour. The man did as asked. Then he came back after a few days to complain about him. Then he came back again and again. The Prophet then decided to have him see the wisdom of harmony with the neighbour. He asked the victim to put his own luggage and items outside his house. The victim did as advised. Soon, a passersby started asking him the reason why he was literally out of his house. He told him his story. The passersby started cursing his neighbour. Hearing this, the neighbour came out and requested him to put his belongings back in the house and promised that from here on, no action of his would be a cause of concern for him. The two became good and happy neighbours.

Short of rights in property, neighbours have the highest rights in Islam and are kept close as family, whatever their religion. For instance, a man is asked not to throw the peels of fruits in front of his house in the dustbin. This is done to save hurt to his neighbour who may not be able to afford similar fruits for his children, who may demand the same in their innocence.

Hygiene

It is important to maintain proper hygiene all the time. We are instructed to perform wudu before prayer and even before going to bed. One day, a person failed to observe this discipline even as he went to offer prayer in a congregation behind the Prophet. Prophet Muhammad was praying salaat-us-subh and reciting Surah Rum from the Quran. He, however, got mixed up with the verses. He completed the prayer and said, 'What is the matter with people who pray with us but do not purify themselves properly? Such people are the ones who make us get mixed up when we recite the Quran.'

So, when we stand up for prayer, we must perform ablution properly, taking care to wash our hands, face and feet properly besides rinsing our mouth. Any mistake in wudu renders our prayer meaningless as we get distracted by foul smells and bad hygiene.

Hide Flaws

All of us make mistakes. That is why Prophet Muhammad told his followers to hide the flaws of anybody they knew. According to Islam, a person who hides the mistakes or blemishes of another person has seventy mistakes of his hidden by Allah.

One sees the Prophet himself practicing this tenet. For example, on one occasion, when a man was guilty of not observing the rules of hygiene while performing prayer behind the Prophet, the Prophet did not reveal his identity in front of other devotees, thus saving him from social ridicule.

Story of the Drunkard

A man used to be fond of the company of the Prophet. He was quite a jester and would make the Prophet laugh. He, however, had a bad habit. He would often get drunk. Then he would be brought before the Prophet, who used to order that he should be whipped so he remembers his mistake.

One day, as the Prophet issued instructions that this jester-drunkard should be whipped, one of the men present there, said, 'O Allah! Curse him!' Hearing this, Prophet Muhammad remarked, 'Do not curse him, for by Allah, all I know of him is that this man loves Allah and His Messenger.' He equated it with helping Shaitan against their brother.

Granted Pardon

Prophet Muhammad did not give up on people even after they had wronged themselves. He always believed that it was up to Allah to give them the right direction. Human beings could only invite people to the path of Allah, not force them or change their hearts. He prayed for his companions, even for those people who went astray. The Prophet's behaviour with the man who was a drunkard is one such instance. When his companions rebuked him and asked if he had forgotten about Allah and His prophet while doing such a sinful deed as drinking which would lead his true senses astray, the Prophet asked his companions to let him go and pray for forgiveness for him! Thus for the Prophet, every man stood a chance of being redeemed from his mistakes and follies, no matter how far he had gone. The Prophet said that it was always possible to seek Allah's pardon even with the worst mistake committed and start afresh.

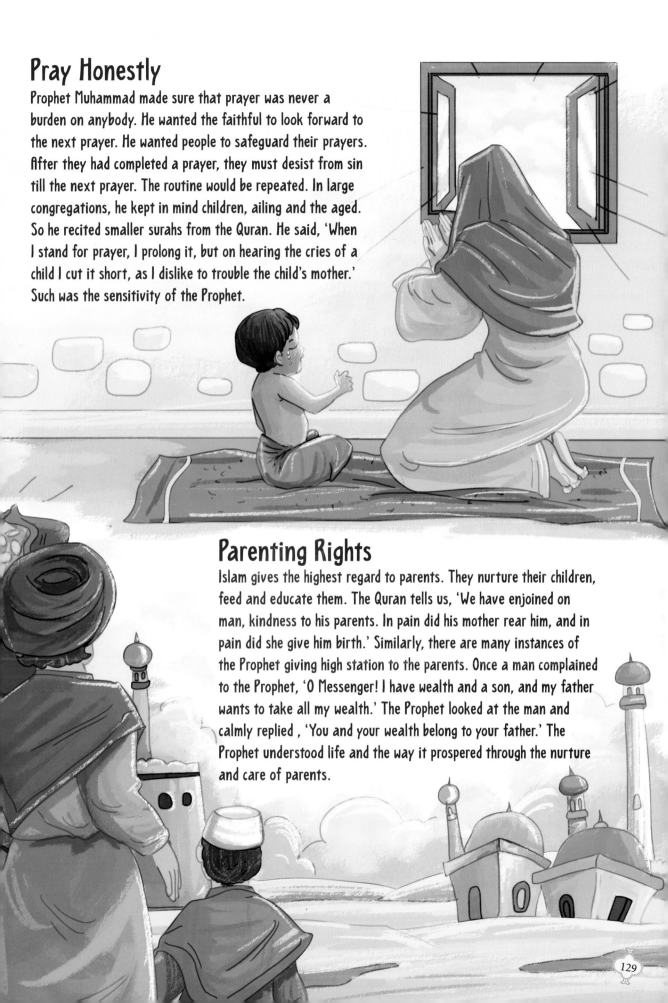

Pray Honestly

Prophet Muhammad made sure that prayer was never a burden on anybody. He wanted the faithful to look forward to the next prayer. He wanted people to safeguard their prayers. After they had completed a prayer, they must desist from sin till the next prayer. The routine would be repeated. In large congregations, he kept in mind children, ailing and the aged. So he recited smaller surahs from the Quran. He said, 'When I stand for prayer, I prolong it, but on hearing the cries of a child I cut it short, as I dislike to trouble the child's mother.' Such was the sensitivity of the Prophet.

Parenting Rights

Islam gives the highest regard to parents. They nurture their children, feed and educate them. The Quran tells us, 'We have enjoined on man, kindness to his parents. In pain did his mother rear him, and in pain did she give him birth.' Similarly, there are many instances of the Prophet giving high station to the parents. Once a man complained to the Prophet, 'O Messenger! I have wealth and a son, and my father wants to take all my wealth.' The Prophet looked at the man and calmly replied , 'You and your wealth belong to your father.' The Prophet understood life and the way it prospered through the nurture and care of parents.

The Way to Paradise

It is said a father's prayer enables one to enter the Jannah. Paradise itself lies at the feet of the mother. Prophet Muhammad said, 'He who wishes to enter the Paradise at the best gate, must please his father and mother.' Every day is parents' day in Islam.

Nobody Is Alone

When nobody is watching, we tend to be naughty. We even commit sins thinking nobody is watching. Similarly, there are times when we feel lonely in the absence of parents and friends. Life just seems lonely without them. Truth is that nobody is ever alone. Allah brought Isa into this world without a father. And when Musa was just a little baby, Allah asked Musa's mother to put him into a chest and let the chest float in the river. Not only did both survive, they also rose to guide mankind. Similarly, Prophet Muhammad lost his father before he was born. He went on to receive the Quran that was guidance to mankind. Nobody is ever alone. Allah is always there watching over us. The Quran tells us, 'Allah sees all that you do.'

Rise in Paradise

The best gift parents can give to their children is good education. And the best thing to leave behind after death are able, compassionate and pious children. Prophet Muhammad said, 'A man will be raised in status in Paradise. He will ask, 'Where did this come from?' It will be said to him, 'By your child asking forgiveness for you'.'

Serve Your Parents

Once Prophet Muhammad was heard by Abu Hurairah saying, 'May he be humiliated. May he be humiliated.' Abu Hurairah, puzzled at the uproar, asked him who he was referring to. Prophet Muhammad replied, 'The one who has one or both his parents live up to old age, yet he does not enter Paradise (by serving them).'

Indeed, treating parents with kindness brings the reward of a pilgrimage. The pleasure of Allah lies in the pleasure of the father and the mother and displeasure of Allah lies in the displeasure of the parents.

Allah Loves All

We love our parents. Our parents love us. But Allah loves us the most. There is a Hadith narrated by Aisha, wife of Prophet Muhammad. She said, 'The Prophet sent (an army unit) under the command of a man who used to lead his companions in prayers. He would finish his recitation with the Surah 112: 'Say O Muhammad: He is Allah, the One.' When they returned from battle, they mentioned that to the Prophet. He said (to them), 'Ask him why he does so.' They asked him. He said, 'I do so because it mentions the qualities of the Beneficent and I love to recite it (in my prayers)'. The Prophet said to them, 'Tell him that Allah loves him'.'

Keep it Simple

Human beings' greed knows no end. There are only a few people who are content with what they have. Most people aspire for more and more, whereas Allah loves those who are content with whatever they might have. Prophet Muhammad said, 'A person who is agreeable and content with limited things, Allah agrees with his small good deeds.' Keep it simple. Keep it small.

Goodness Is Rewarded

Allah is Beneficent. He is Merciful. So a man who commits a sin is punished only for that sin. But a man who does a good deed gets the reward for ten good deeds. Said Prophet Muhammad, 'Whoever recites a letter from the Book of Allah (the Quran) he will be credited with a good deed. A good deed gets a ten-fold reward. I do not say that Alif-Lam-Meem is one letter but Alif is a letter, Lam is a letter and Meem is a letter.' Indeed, the best is he who learns the Quran and teaches it.

Remembering Allah

We all remember Allah in times of difficulty. For example, when our exams are round the corner or we are finding it difficult to solve some problems, we think of Him. Our beloved Prophet, though, advised us to remember Allah all the time, both in good times and in challenging times. He said, 'Remember Allah during times of ease and He will remember you during times of difficulty.'

Love for the Girl Child

When Prophet Muhammad brought a message of peace and brotherhood to all, the Arab world was completely divided and full of strife. Most girls did not enjoy the right to life. He gave them not just the right to life, but also the right to education and the right in their father's property. The Prophet loved all children, but he loved girls a little bit more. He said once, 'Be fair and just in terms of the gifts you offer your children. If I were to give preference to any (gender over the other), I would have preferred females over males (in terms of giving gifts).' Such was the love in his heart for the girl child.

Fatimah and the Prophet

Prophet Muhammad used to love his children a lot. There is a tradition according to which he would stand up when his daughter Fatimah would enter the room.

He would kiss her hand too. He is reported to have said, 'Fatimah is part of me. Whatever upsets her, upsets me and whatever harms her, harms me.' It shows that there is no room for favouring or loving sons more than daughters.

Tawaf

A man was doing a tawaf (going around) of the Kaaba with his aged mother on his back. Caliph Umar saw this. The man asked him if he had done his duty towards his mother. Caliph Umar replied, 'No, not even for one contraction (of labour pain).' He then added, 'But you have done good and Allah will reward you tremendously for the little you could do.' No matter what we do, we cannot compensate our mother for even a single night she spent awake for us.

Reward after Death

He who has taken a breath shall taste death too. When a man dies, the account of his deeds is closed too. There is one exception. It is reported that the Prophet said, 'When the son of Adam dies (all mankind is progeny of Adam) all his actions cease, except three: a continual charity, beneficial knowledge, and righteous children who pray for their parent.' So, setting up a school, building a mosque or getting an orphan or poor child free education are all part of deeds, which continue to pay dividends even after death.

Seek Knowledge

It is obligatory on every person to seek knowledge. The very first word of the Quran is 'Iqra', (read). The Quran too talks of 'Rabbi zidni ilma' (O Lord! Increase me in knowledge). Prophet Muhammad regarded the ink of a scholar's pen to be mightier than the blood of a martyr. He said,

'He who walks in search of knowledge has his path to Paradise made easy by Allah.'

Guarantee to Paradise

Everybody wants to enter Paradise and enjoy the fruits there, but few are ready to work for it. Prophet Muhammad gave a guarantee of entry to Paradise to an individual who does six things: Speak the truth when you talk; keep a promise when you make it; fulfill your trust; avoid sexual immorality; lower your gaze in modesty and restrain your hands from injustice.

The Last Sermon

Prophet Muhammad laid out the blueprint for the future with his last sermon. He talked of equality of races in his sermon. He said, 'All mankind is from Adam and Eve. An Arab has no superiority over a non-Arab, nor a non-Arab has any superiority over an Arab; also, a white has no superiority over a black nor does a black have any superiority over a white except by piety (taqwa) and good action. Learn that every Muslim is a brother to every Muslim, and that the Muslims constitute one brotherhood. Nothing shall be legitimate to a Muslim which belongs to a fellow Muslim unless it be given freely and willingly.'

In the same sermon, he gave responsibility to each Muslim to pass on the message to others, one generation to the next. He said, 'All those who listen to me shall pass on my words to the others and those to others again; and may the last ones understand my words better than those who listen to me directly.'

Usury

Islam forbids taking or giving of interest. The Quran regards a man who indulges in this practice to be at war with the Lord and His Messenger. Verse 279, Surah Baqarah says, 'And if you do not, then be warned of war (against you) from Allah and His Messenger. And if you repent, then you shall have your principal (without interest). Wrong not, and you shall not be wronged.'

The Prophet too, in his last sermon, emphasised it. He said, 'Allah has forbidden you to take usury (interest). Therefore, all interest obligations shall henceforth be waived. Your capital, however, is yours to keep. You will neither inflict nor suffer inequity. Allah has judged that there shall be no interest and that all the interest due to Abbas ibn Abdal Mutatlib (Prophet's uncle) shall be waived.'

Caliph Usman's Words

Caliph Usman, one of the four caliphs, said, 'Four things were useless. They were: knowledge without practice; wealth without expenditure in the ways of Allah; piety for the sake of show (prompted by feeling of worldliness), and a long life with no stock of good deeds.'

Incidentally, Caliph Usman used to love to feed the hungry, clothe the naked, and read and teach the Quran.

Caliph Abu Bakr's Teachings

Caliph Abu Bakr was a man of calm disposition. He took forward the teachings of Prophet Muhammad. He is reported to have laid emphasis on knowledge and education. He said, 'Without knowledge, action is useless. And knowledge without action is futile.' He is also reported to have once advised the faithful, 'The more knowledge you have, the greater will be your fear of Allah.' To prevent people from sinning, he said, 'Sin committed by a young man is bad, but an old person committing a sin is worse.'

Caliph Ali's Advice

Caliph Ali was the husband of Fatimah. Thus he was the son-in-law of Prophet Muhammad. Realising that this world was made for man but man was not built for this world, he advised the faithful to keep their focus on Hereafter. He is reported to have said, 'Do for this life as if you will live forever. Do for the afterlife as if you die tomorrow.' In other words, he wanted us to be ready for death at any given moment and emphasised keeping our positive deeds higher on scale in comparison to our sins.

Following the Prophet

The Quran tells us that whoever follows the Messenger, follows the Quran. It talks of him as an excellent role model. Following the Prophet's practices, his Sunnah is an obligation to all. There is an old saying, 'The loss of religion starts with the abandonment of the Sunnah. Just as a rope breaks, so does religion vanish with one by one abandoning the Sunnah.'

Respecting Life and Abundance

One day, the Prophet came out of the house and found two of his beloved companions, Abu Bakr and Umar standing outside. He was surprised to see them, and asked them why they were out at that hour. They explained that they had not eaten for a long time and hunger had driven them out. Prophet Muhammad replied, 'By Him in Whose hands is my life, the same cause has brought me out that has brought both of you out. So come along.' The three of them then went to the house of an Ansar man, a local inhabitant of Medina. He had gone to fetch some sweet water. They were welcomed at his house. When he came home, he was delighted to see the three of them, saying, 'There is no one who has more honoured guests today than I have.' The Ansar man then went out to bring some dates for his guests. In his open-hearted, generous wish to serve his guests the best, he was about to slaughter a goat when he was stopped by the Prophet. The Prophet commanded him not to kill a milk-bearing animal. They helped themselves to dates and milk. When the three of them had had their fill, the Prophet reminded his companions, 'By Him in Whose hands is my life, you will be called to account for these bounties on the Day of Judgement.'

Muadh in Yemen

Once the Prophet sent his representative Muadh, to Yemen. As Muadh prepared to leave, the Prophet asked him, 'How will you judge? (disputes among people)' Muadh replied, 'I will judge according to what is in Allah's Book.' The Prophet asked, 'If it is not in Allah's Book?' Muadh answered, 'Then I will judge with the Sunnah of the Messenger of Allah.' The Prophet asked him, 'If it is not in the Sunnah of Messenger of Allah?' The man stated, 'I will endeavour to make Ijtihad (make an attempt to arrive at the right judgement).'

The Legacy of Caliph Umar

Prophet Muhammad regarded Umar among the best. He is reported to have said, 'If some Prophet had been proposed by Allah after me, it would have been Umar bin Khattab.' The Prophet had great love for him. Once in his dream, the Prophet saw that he had a bowl of milk from which he drank, the other he gave to Umar. That is because his companion Umar had a reputation for honesty and truthfulness. The Prophet said of him, 'I see that Shaitaan, either from jinns or humans, runs away from Umar.'

Abu Bakr and Umar's Dispute

The companions of the Prophet used to have their share of misunderstandings and quarrels. Once, two of his closest companions who later became caliphs, had a quarrel. There was a dispute between Abu Bakr and Umar. Abu Bakr made Umar angry. So Umar went away fuming. Abu Bakr followed him. There was another reason for why he was following Umar. He wanted to seek forgiveness from him and not to say anything hurtful.Umar, however, was not calmed by that and slammed the door on Abu Bakr's face. At this, Abu Bakr went to the messenger of Allah, and said, 'This companion of yours has got me involved in a dispute.' Then Umar regretted his action, and made peace by saying 'Salaam.' Abu Bakr claimed that he was wrong. The Prophet initially got angry, then reminded everybody of Abu Bakr's truthful nature, telling them that when nobody believed in him, Abu Bakr did. All was well.

وَعَلَيْكُمُ السَّلَام

Jamaat

Prophet Muhammad was sensitive to the needs of the specially-abled. Their interests were dear to his heart. Once, a visually challenged man came to meet him. He did not live close to a mosque and had no one to guide him along the way. In those days, the roads were uneven and not safe. It was difficult for him to reach the mosque on his own. The man asked Prophet Muhammad for exemption from the congregational prayer in the mosque. He wanted to pray at home. Prophet Muhammad granted him permission to do so. Then, just as the man turned back and started walking back home, the Prophet called him and asked, 'Do you hear the call for prayer, the athaan?' The man replied, 'Yes.' Then the Prophet withdrew the exemption, saying, 'Then respond to it.' With this decision, he made it clear that there were no exemptions from jamaat, not even for the specially-abled.

Seeking Forgiveness

A companion revealed that he had heard the Prophet say, 'Allah is my witness that I seek forgiveness of Allah and turn to Him more than seventy times a day.' He used to ask his followers to turn to Allah and seek forgiveness of Him. It is said that Allah is more pleased with the repentance of a servant of His, than would be the one who were to lose his camel in a desert and then suddenly find it.

What he meant was that just as a man who had lost his camel in a vast desert would have reacted on finding his camel again, in the same way Allah is pleased when a man who had gone astray comes back to Him seeking His forgiveness.

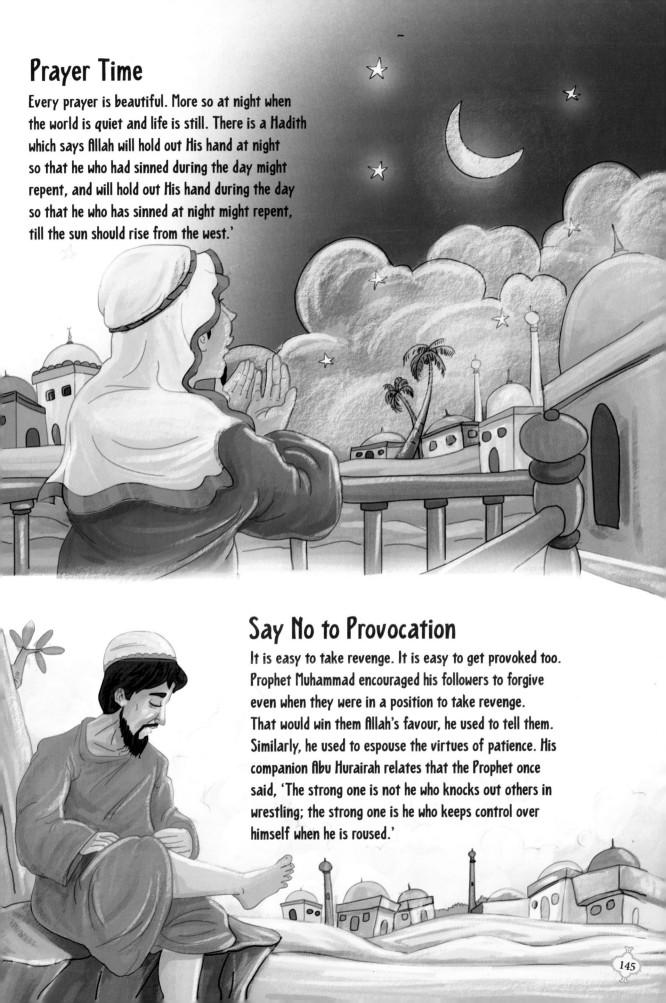

Prayer Time

Every prayer is beautiful. More so at night when the world is quiet and life is still. There is a Hadith which says Allah will hold out His hand at night so that he who had sinned during the day might repent, and will hold out His hand during the day so that he who has sinned at night might repent, till the sun should rise from the west.'

Say No to Provocation

It is easy to take revenge. It is easy to get provoked too. Prophet Muhammad encouraged his followers to forgive even when they were in a position to take revenge. That would win them Allah's favour, he used to tell them. Similarly, he used to espouse the virtues of patience. His companion Abu Hurairah relates that the Prophet once said, 'The strong one is not he who knocks out others in wrestling; the strong one is he who keeps control over himself when he is roused.'

145

Remedy for Anger

When angry, seek refuge in Allah. There are times when we do get angry, times when we want to shout and scream, hit and slap. At all such times, we are advised to observe restraint by the Prophet. It was related by a companion of the Prophet, Sulaiman Ibn Surad that once he was sitting with the Prophet when two men started quarrelling amongst themselves. One of the men went red in the face. At that time, the Prophet said, 'If he were to repeat a phrase, I know he would be rid of the condition in which he finds himself.' And what was that phrase? It was a simple phrase which meant, 'I seek refuge with Allah against Satan, the rejected one.' So the man was told to repeat what the Prophet had advised to get rid of his ill will and bout of anger.

اَعُوْذُ بِاللّٰهِ مِنَ الشَّيْطَانِ الرَّجِيْم

Discrimination

The Prophet wanted the faithful to be steadfast at the time of crisis and never to give up but bear with patience whatever befalls them. During the time of the Prophet, a man from the Ansar tribe (natives of Medina who helped the Prophet and his companions) came to him and asked, 'Will you not appoint me to public office as you have appointed so and so?' He replied, 'You will experience discrimination after I am gone but be steadfast till you meet me in Paradise.' The Prophet elaborated to the companions, 'After I am gone, you will experience discrimination and will observe things that you will disapprove.' So he was asked a way out. The Prophet said, 'Discharge your obligations and supplicate before Allah for your rights.' Doing your duty well irrespective of the situation will, in time, end discrimination and gain you respect.'

146

Divine Inspiration

Prophet Muhammad once said, 'Every Prophet was given miracles so people believed, but what I have been given is Divine Inspiration that Allah has revealed to me. So I hope that my followers will outnumber the followers of the other Prophets on the Day of Resurrection.'

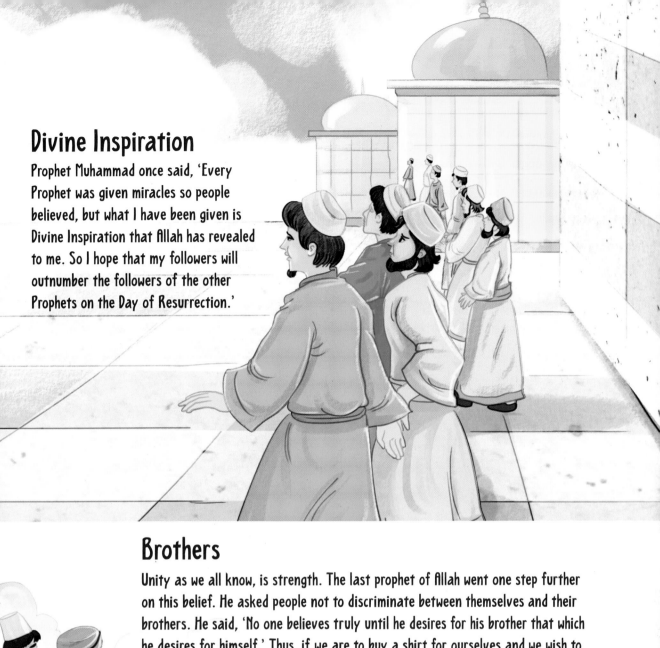

Brothers

Unity as we all know, is strength. The last prophet of Allah went one step further on this belief. He asked people not to discriminate between themselves and their brothers. He said, 'No one believes truly until he desires for his brother that which he desires for himself.' Thus, if we are to buy a shirt for ourselves and we wish to gift one to our brother, we should see to it that it is in no way inferior to what we would love to use. Our Prophet said, 'Be not envious of each other. Do not make fictitious bids at auctions, do not grudge, do not turn away from each other, do not make an offering during a pending transaction and become servants of Allah, brothers to each other. A Muslim is a brother of a Muslim. He does not wrong him or look down upon him, or humiliate him. Righteousness is a matter of the heart. Everything of a Muslim is forbidden to a Muslim; his blood, his property, his honour.'

Abuse of Parents

Prophet Muhammad considered abuse of parents as a major sin. 'Association of other prophets with Allah, disobedience to parents and telling a lie or giving false evidence is sin.' He continued, 'Abusing one's parents is a major sin.' So a companion asked, how is it possible that a person can abuse his own parents? He was shocked to know that parents could be abused.

The Prophet replied, 'Yes, if one's father abuses another person's father, the latter would in turn abuse his father. If he abuses another person's mother, the latter would abuse his own mother.' This cycle of hatred would continue till one practices patience and compassion in their lives, as suggested by the Quran.

Continuing the Tradition with Elders

It is considered a great virtue to be good to one's father's friends. It is something we are expected to do even after our parents pass away. It was narrated by Abdullah Ibn Dinar that once Abdullah Ibn Umar was travelling to Makkah. He got tired riding a camel. So he decided to use a donkey. When he was riding his donkey with a turban over his head in the desert, he saw a local Arab man pass by. He recognised him and promptly gave him the donkey to ride. He gave him his turban too. Some companions wondered why had he done that, giving his means of transport to the local man and put himself in discomfort? He replied, 'I have heard the Prophet say, 'It is of the highest virtue that a person should be benevolent towards the families of the friends of his father after his death. This man's father was a friend of my father.'

Prophet's Love for His First Wife

Prophet Muhammad married Khadijah when he was twenty-five. She was with him when the first revelation came down to the Prophet. She was with him in the difficult years when the Prophet and his companions were persecuted for their beliefs. The Prophet loved her enormously, so much so that even after she passed away, he used to care for her friends and her sister. It is narrated by Ayshah, 'I did not envy any of the wives of the Prophet as much as I envied Khadijah, though I had never seen her. The Prophet would mention her often. When a goat was slaughtered, he would cut its pieces and send them to Khadijah's friends. Sometimes, I would say to him, 'You talk of her as if there never was a woman in the world beside Khadijah, and he would say, 'She was such and such'.' The Prophet would send gifts to her friends. Once when his wife's sister wanted to visit him, he could not help recall the manners and ways of his wife. The visit reminded him of his dear departed wife.

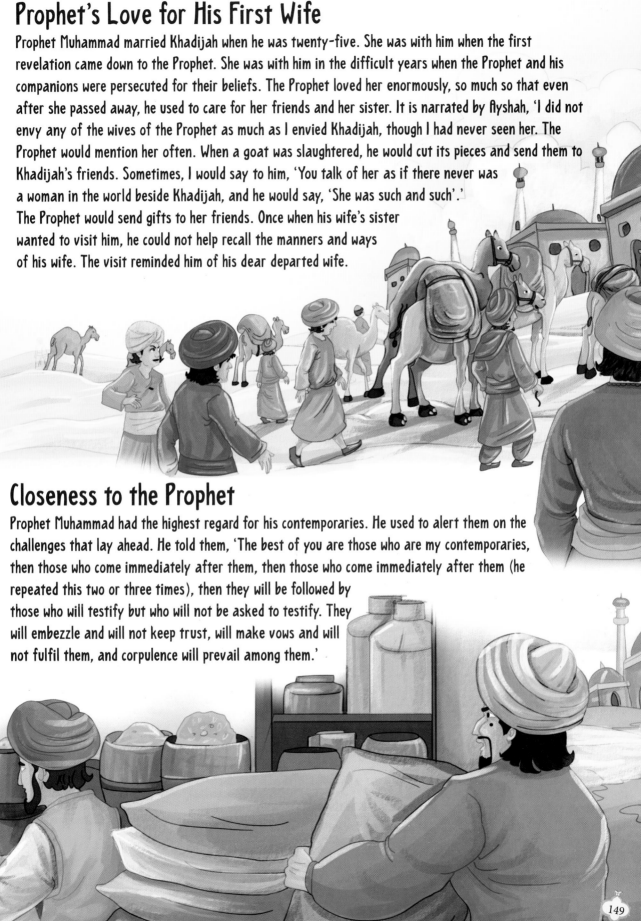

Closeness to the Prophet

Prophet Muhammad had the highest regard for his contemporaries. He used to alert them on the challenges that lay ahead. He told them, 'The best of you are those who are my contemporaries, then those who come immediately after them, then those who come immediately after them (he repeated this two or three times), then they will be followed by those who will testify but who will not be asked to testify. They will embezzle and will not keep trust, will make vows and will not fulfil them, and corpulence will prevail among them.'

Abu Hurairah and the Cup

Abu Hurairah was going through the worst pangs of hunger. He had to tie a stone around his stomach to make hunger bearable. One day, the Prophet saw him in this condition and instructed Abu Hurairah to follow him. Prophet Muhammad reached home and found a cup of milk. He asked about it and was told that it was given by one of the grateful as a present for the Prophet. He immediately called Abu Hurairah over. To his surprise though, he asked Abu Hurairah to join him in company at the lounge where men who had no family or property stayed. These men were regarded as guests of Muslims and it was the Prophet's practice to pass on anything he received as charity to them. Abu Hurairah though driven by hunger, for once, was unsure of the move. He did not believe that anything would be left for him after the cup passed over to the men at the lounge. The cup passed from one man to another. Each had his fill. Finally, only the Prophet and Abu Hurairah were left. The Prophet asked Abu Hurairah to drink. He drank to his fill till he could find absolutely no room for more! Then the Prophet too drank what was left of it. The Prophet pronounced the name of Allah and finally finished the overflowing cup of milk.

Being Good to Guests

A guest is a sign of a blessing. Fortunate is the house where a guest arrives. Abu Shuraih Khalid related that he heard the Prophet say, 'He who believes in Allah and the Last Day should honour his guest according to his right.' He was asked what his right was. The messenger of Allah replied, 'A day and a night, and hospitality for three days. That which might be beyond this, is charity.' A guest too should try not to stay on for more than three days.

On Portraiture

Prophet Muhammad forbade making portraits. In a Hadith, Ayesha, one of the wives of the Prophet reveals, 'The Prophet returned from a journey and in his absence I had screened a platform in front of my house with a curtain on which there were pictures. When the Prophet saw it, he was drained of colour, and said, 'Ayesha, the worst chastised by Allah on the Day of Judgement will be those who copy Allah's creation'. So I cut it up and made one or two pillow covers from it.'

Divine Delight

It is best to finish food to the last morsel, the last grain. In fact, Prophet Muhammad asked the believers to lick their fingers and clean their vessels at the conclusion of a meal. According to a Hadith, he said, 'You do not know which part of the food is more richly blessed. If any of you should happen to drop a morsel, he should pick it up, clean it of dust and eat it; and not leave it for Satan. Nor should you wipe your hands with a napkin without licking the food off your fingers, for you know not which part of the food is richly blessed.'

Hold on to Prophet's Practice

Ayesha was the youngest wife of the Prophet. As she was much younger to the Prophet, she outlived him by many years. It helped her spread the message of the Prophet for many years after he had left this world. In fact, often the companions of the Prophet would recall a certain Hadith of the Prophet as having been told through Ayesha. A companion Irabaah Ibn Sariah recalled that once the Prophet made a particularly moving speech. The Prophet and the companions got pretty emotional. So much so that the companions believed it was his final address to them! They begged him to say some more. Upon their request, the Prophet told them to be always mindful of their duty to Allah and their duty to those in positions of authority, whatever their race. It won't be easy, the Prophet warned them, but they had a ready reckoner with them: They had to abide by the practices of the Prophet, and shun any innovation in the name of the Prophet's teachings. 'Hold fast to my practice, and the practice of my rightly guided successors. Hold on to it by your hind teeth,' the Prophet advised them.

A Short, Sincere Prayer

Allah loves moderation and consistency. The Prophet used to emphasise consistency even if it was for the smallest of good deeds. Similarly, he was not in favour of any act of worship that would tire out the believers. Once he came home when his wife Ayesha had a woman as a guest. His wife praised the guest saying, she is the only one whose long-drawn-out salaat is much-talked about. Prophet turned around to the guest and said, 'You are required to do only that much which you can carry out easily. Allah does not tire of you until you tire of Him. Allah likes that spiritual exercise best which a worshipper can carry out diligently.'

Teaching the Quran without a Fee

Prophet Muhammad said, 'Read the Quran and act by it. And do not abandon it, do not exceed its limits, do not eat with it (i.e. money) and do not seek more by using it.' In other words, it is not proper to earn money for teaching the Quran.

153

Community of the Faithful

After the Prophet had gone on Mairaj (a nightlong journey to heaven and back), there was a lot of curiosity among the companions about it. While many locals wondered on the possibility and some openly questioned it, the companions had complete faith in him, and believed every word of his. They all wanted to know what the Prophet had seen. So one day, the Prophet decided to share his experience with them. He said, 'I was shown many peoples. I saw a Prophet who had only a small party with him, some Prophets had only one or two persons with them, and some did not have even one. Then suddenly, I saw a huge assemblage and I imagined that they were my people, but I was told, 'This is Musa and his people.'

As the Prophet continued to recall his spiritual journey in the course of which he saw both heaven and hell, he said, 'I was told, 'Lift your eyes'. I looked and saw a great number of people. I was told, 'These are your people and of them there are seventy thousand who shall enter Paradise without any acounting or suffering.'

The Prophet's account left the companions wondering if they would be among those seventy thousand people or not. After some time, the Prophet came back, and and asked, 'What are you discussing?' The companions told him the truth. He told them, the ones who will enter Paradise without any accounting would be the ones who did not make any charms, nor did they seek omens but they put their trust only in Allah. Hearing this, Ukasha, a companion, stood up and said, 'Supplicate to Allah that He makes me one of them.' The Prophet said, 'You are one of them.'

The Devout Murderer

A man who had killed as many as ninety-nine people, inquired who was the most learned person on this earth. He was told to meet a monk. He went to the monk and confessed that he had killed ninety-nine people, and if there was a possibility of repentance for him. The monk said, 'No'. Upon this, he murdered the monk too. Thus he completed a century of murders. He regretted it and wanted to know if there was a chance if his repentance could be accepted. This time he went to a savant. The savant said, 'Yes,' adding, 'What can stand between you and repentance? Proceed to such and such place. In it you will find people who worship Allah. Join them in worship, and do not return to this land of evil.' The man was truly regretful of his actions now. He wanted to atone for all the wrong deeds he had done. The dead were gone, but he could at least try to find God's pardon. But after what all he had done, he was not sure. Still, the man started walking towards the land suggested by the savant. He hoped to reach it soon and atone for his mistakes. He had covered only half the distance, when he died. Now, the question was whether his expression of regret had been accepted by the Almighty or not. After all, he had killed a hundred people. But then, he was truly sorry for his actions.

A debate ensued between the angels of mercy and the angels of torment. The angels of mercy contended that he had returned to Allah as a penitent man. The angels of torment, however, argued that he had never done a good deed. As they debated, there arrived an angel in human form. The angels made him the arbiter between them. He directed them to measure the distance between the two lands, the land of evil and the land of the devout. A measurement was carried out and he was found to be closer to the land of the devout. The angels of mercy took charge over him. He was pardoned because he had expressed true regret for his actions.

The King and the Magician

There was a king. At his court was a famous magician. With the passage of years, the magician grew old and wanted to pass on his knowledge to the young. The king sent him an able young man. On the young man's way to the magician, there sat a monk. The young man was enamoured by the monk and sat down to listen to him preaching. The monk left a mark on the young man. Every time he would go to the magician, he would spend some time with the monk. The magician could not tolerate this and beat him up. The young man complained to the monk about this. The monk told him to tell the magician, 'My people have detained me. Why are you afraid of your people? Tell them the monk detained me.' The young man did as was told. This went on for a while. One day, the young man noticed that a big beast blocked the road and nobody could pass. The young man thought to himself that today he would find out, who was more powerful—the monk or the magician. He took a stone and prayed, 'Lord! If the way of the monk is more to your liking than the way of the magician, then bring about the death of this beast so people can pass through.' People did away with the beast. The young man went to the monk and related the incident to him. The monk replied, 'You have become better than I and I conceive that you have arrived at a stage when you will get into trouble. Should that happen, do not disclose my whereabouts.'

The young man had gained powers and started helping people, curing them of leprosy and blindness. His fame reached the king who by then had become blind. The king offered him lavish gifts if he cured him. The young man told him, 'I cannot heal anybody. It is Allah who bestows healing. If you believe in Allah, I will pray for you and He will heal you.' The king began believing in Allah and Allah cured him of blindness.

The young man went to the king and sat beside him. The king asked him on who had restored his eyesight. He answered, 'My God.' Upon this, the king asked, did he have another god besides Him? The young man said, 'Allah is the only One. He is your God and my God. He is everyone's God.'

In the Name of Allah

Prophet Muhammad was particular that there should be no association of any deity with Allah. He prohibited asking for anything in the name of Allah, anything except Paradise. All good deeds were to happen in Allah's name. He is reported to have said, 'Grant asylum to him who begs for it in the name of Allah, and give to him who asks in the name of Allah, and respond to him who invites you, and compensate him who is benevolent towards you, but if you cannot afford it, go on praying for him till you are satisfied that you have compensated him adequately.'

No Evil or Superstition

There was no scope for superstition or bad omen in the grammar of the Prophet. He said, 'There is no infection and no bad omen but I am pleased with good augury.' His companions asked him what good augury was. He replied, 'A good word.' This meant that good words and intentions were all that were real, not superstitions or bad omens.

Fatimah's Whispers

Once upon a time, all the wives of the Prophet had gathered around him. Just then, his daughter Fatimah walked in. The Prophet warmly welcomed her and asked her to be seated close to him. He then whispered something into her ear. Fatimah started weeping on hearing this. The Prophet saw her in this condition and whispered again into her ear. This time, she smiled on hearing his words. Fatimah did not reveal what the Prophet had shared with her. When he had breathed his last, his wife Ayesha prevailed upon Fatimah to tell her what had transpired that day. Fatimah said, 'When he whispered to me the first time, he told me that every year Jibrail used to hear him recite the Quran and then recite it back to him. This time he had done it twice. He said, "I see that my time is approaching. Then be mindful of your duty to Allah and be steadfast, for I shall be an excellent forerunner for you." On this, I cried as you saw. When he perceived my grief, he whispered to me the second time, and said, "Fatimah, are you not pleased that you will be the first among the believing women?" on which I smiled.'

The Keeper of the Prophet's Secret

When Hafsah, daughter of Umar, became a widow, her father decided to find her a new match. First he went to Usman with the proposal. Usman sought some time to consider the matter. After a few days, he excused himself from the proposal. Then the father went to Abu Bakr and offered to marry Hafsah to him. Abu Bakr kept quiet. Umar was upset. After a few days, he met Prophet Muhammad who asked for Hafsah's hand in marriage. Hafsah was married to him. Later Umar met Abu Bakr who told him, 'You might have been upset with me over the proposal of Hafsah.' When Umar replied in the affirmative, Abu Bakr revealed, 'The only thing that stood in the way was that Prophet Muhammad had mentioned her and I could not disclose the Prophet's secret. Had the Prophet not made the offer, I would have agreed to the proposal.'

Life in This World

Once the Prophet sent Abu Ubaidah to Bahrain to collect toll tax. He returned with the money. The Ansar (local men of Madinah) heard about it and became happy that they may have a chance too. Next morning, they joined the Prophet in Fajr prayer. Once the prayer was over, they presented themselves before him. The Prophet understood the purpose of their presence. He said, 'Rejoice, and hope for that which will please you. It is not poverty that I apprehend for you. What I apprehend for you is that you might begin to desire the world as they desired it and it might destroy you as it destroyed them.'

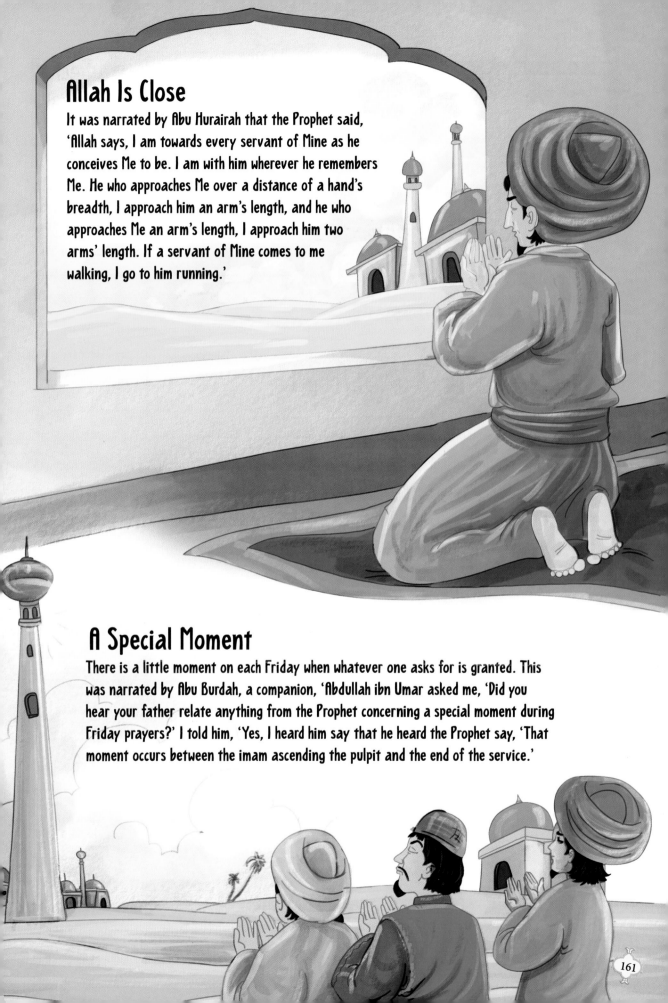

Allah Is Close

It was narrated by Abu Hurairah that the Prophet said, 'Allah says, I am towards every servant of Mine as he conceives Me to be. I am with him wherever he remembers Me. He who approaches Me over a distance of a hand's breadth, I approach him an arm's length, and he who approaches Me an arm's length, I approach him two arms' length. If a servant of Mine comes to me walking, I go to him running.'

A Special Moment

There is a little moment on each Friday when whatever one asks for is granted. This was narrated by Abu Burdah, a companion, 'Abdullah ibn Umar asked me, 'Did you hear your father relate anything from the Prophet concerning a special moment during Friday prayers?' I told him, 'Yes, I heard him say that he heard the Prophet say, 'That moment occurs between the imam ascending the pulpit and the end of the service.'

Head Early for Friday Prayers

Prophet Muhammad explained the many gifts of Friday to a believer. He told them, 'He who takes a full bath on Friday and repairs early to the mosque is as if he had sacrificed a camel for winning Allah's pleasure. He who proceeds to the mosque after him is as if he had sacrificed a cow. He who goes after him is as if he had sacrificed a chicken. And he who goes last is as if he has sacrificed an egg. When the imam arrives, the angels gather in to listen to his address.'

No to Lies

The Quran tells us to cross-check a piece of information which comes out of our mouths lest we regret it later. The Hadiths make the need for investigation before passing on any crucial news. According to a Hadith, the Prophet said, 'It is enough to make a man a liar that he should go on repeating all that he might hear.' Once a woman asked him about her co-wife saying, 'O messenger of Allah! I have a co-wife. Would it be sinful if I were to pretend that my husband had given me something which he had not given me?' He replied, 'One who pretends having received something that was not given to him (or her) is like one who wears two garments of falsehood.'

Ways of Charity

The best charity is the one where one gives with one hand and the other hand does not get to know. When a man puts his hand into his pocket, he takes the money and gives it to a needy person without the eyes seeing it. The Prophet asked us not to look into the eyes of the beneficiary of the charity for he might be feeling grateful towards us. Our looking at him might just embarrass him. So the best charity is the one done quietly without anybody knowing it. 'This is an immediate appreciation of a believer's good deed.'

Decent Conversation

Islam insists on clean conversation, shunning cuss words. Once, a few men were sitting at a platform in front of their house. They were indulging in some malicious gossip when the Prophet happened to pass by. On seeing them, he stopped and asked, 'Why do you sit along the street?' The men replied that they were doing no harm to anybody, only conversing among themselves. At this the Prophet responded, 'If you must, discharge your obligation, namely, guard your eyes, respond to salutation and converse decently.' A tongue which is used to sing praises of Allah is not meant to be used for speaking cuss words.

Fighting Brothers

Muslims are known to be brothers to each other. What is not as well known, is that a Muslim is not supposed to fight another Muslim. According to a Hadith, the Prophet was once asked about a case of two Muslims who fought each other, picking up their swords in extreme anger. In the fight, one of the men was killed. The Prophet said, both will end up in Hell. Upon this, he was asked, that it is understandable that the man who killed will go to Hell. Why would the man who died in the fight end up in Hell? After all, he was the victim. The Prophet explained, 'The other was also eager to kill his opponent.'

He continued, 'When one prays for one's brother, the angel says, Ameen, and for you the same.'

Allah Is All

All prophets have been subjected to torment. They have been ridiculed and expelled. Yet, they never lost faith in Allah. They all regarded Allah to be sufficient in the face of mounting odds. When Prophet Ibrahim was thrown into the fire, his last words were, 'Sufficient for me is Allah, and an excellent Guardian is He.' So did Prophet Muhammad when he was told, 'People have mustered against you, so fear them.' This only added to the faith of the Prophet and his followers. He said, 'Sufficient for us is Allah and an excellent Guardian is He.'

حَسْبُنَا اللهُ وَنِعْمَ الْوَكِيلُ

Write off Debts

The Quran asks the well off people to give more time to people to return the money they would have borrowed from them or even to write off the loan completely. It was narrated by Abu Qatadah that the Prophet said, 'If anyone would like Allah to save him from the hardships of the Day of Resurrection, he should give more time to his debtor who is short of money, or remit the debt altogether.'

Maintaining Relations

We are all expected to maintain all ties. Be good to neighbours. Be good to classmates and to strangers and fellow travellers on bus, train or airplane. The Prophet wanted us to give due to all relationships and never cut off ties. He once said, 'He who cuts off ties with blood relations will not enter Paradise.'

Praying Properly

A man entered the mosque and offered prayer. The Prophet was sitting in a far corner. The man initially did not notice him. Then he went up to greet him. The Prophet asked him to repeat his prayer, 'Go back and pray, for you have not prayed.' The man went back and offered prayers again. The process was repeated. Then he asked the Prophet to teach him the right way of prayer. The Prophet told him, 'When you stand up for prayer, do wudu properly. Then face the qiblah and say takbeer. Then recite whatever is easy for you from the Quran. Then bow until you are at ease in rukoo. Then stand up until your back is completely straight. Then prostrate until you are at ease in sujood. Then sit up until you are at ease with sitting. Then prostrate again until you are at ease in sujood. Then sit up again until you are at ease. Do all this in prayer.'

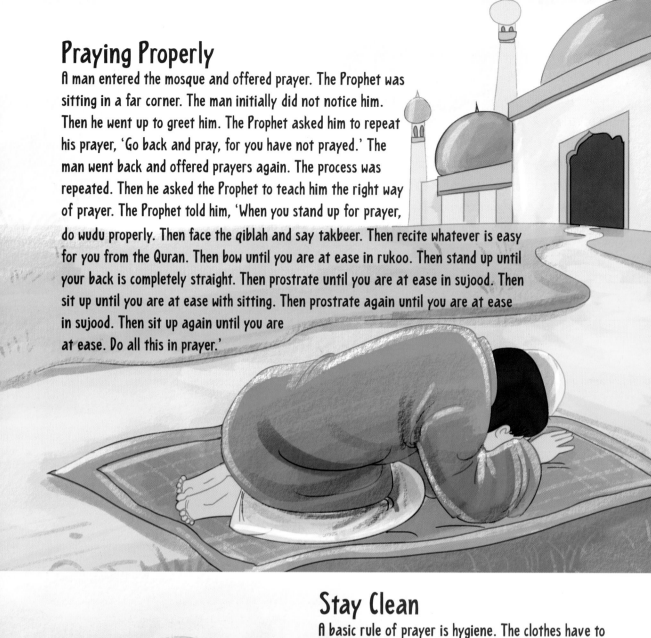

Stay Clean

A basic rule of prayer is hygiene. The clothes have to be absolutely clean, no impurities should be attached to clothes, especially no human excreta. Then wudu or ablution has to be done properly, leaving no hand, foot or a part of the face unwashed. A man once did his wudu but a little portion of his foot was not washed. It remained dry. The Prophet noticed this as he was passing by. He sent him back to do wudu properly again. He did as asked and then was allowed to pray.

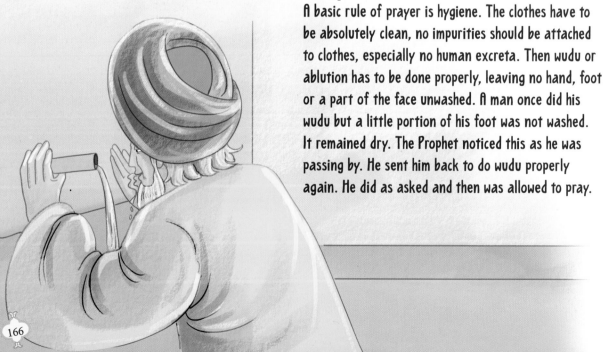

Wishing Others

Prophet Muhammad sat at the top of the Valley. A man came to him with some milk, yogurt and other edible things. Seeing the Prophet he rushed straight to him to present the offerings. He forgot to wish the Prophet. The Prophet asked him to go back, say 'Assalam o alaikum' and then meet him. He, then, did as asked and wished the Prophet peace before starting the conversation.

Making Amends

There are times when we end up hurting others with our action or words. While that should be avoided at all cost, in case we end up hurting those close to us without being aware, there is always scope to make amends in Islam. Once, a man came to the Prophet. He pledged allegiance to him and offered to migrate with him. 'I have come to make hijrah with you. I have left my parents weeping in the process,' he said. The Prophet asked him to go back to his parents, make them smile the way he had made them weep. That was kaffarah or expiation for his mistake, which is a beautiful way of making amends.

Allah Knows

Once Prophet Muhammad visited a companion and sat on his bed. Some girls were playing the daff (hand-held drum) and singing songs in praise of those who had been killed at Badr. One of the girls announced, 'Among us is the Prophet who knows the future.' The Prophet said, 'Do not say that. Say what you were saying before.' He meant that nobody knows the future except Allah so one doesn't need to spread such a rumour.

A Wish on Sneezing

A man sat next to Umar. He sneezed, and said, 'Alhamdulillahi wal-salaam Ala Rasoolallah (Praise be to Allah and peace be upon the Prophet).' Umar corrected him and said that this was not how the Prophet had taught them. He told him that on sneezing, one should instead say, 'Al-hamdu Lillahi 'ala Kulli Haal (Praise be to Allah whatever the circumstances).'

Men of the Cave

The people of Makkah were pushed by the Jews and Christians to ask the Prophet if he knew about the men who stayed in a cave for long years even as a dog stood guard. They wanted to test his knowledge about the matters of which the desert Arabs were ignorant. The Prophet was helped by Allah to give the right answer with the revelation of Surah Kahf in the Quran.

But who were the people in the cave? They were men who believed in Allah but were persecuted for their belief. They took refuge in a cave. As they were running away from hostile people, a dog chased them. Later, as they went off to sleep in the big cave, the dog stood guard. Allah took care of them in the cave. 'When the sun rose, it moved away from their cave. When it set, it turned away from it to the left. The men stayed secure in the spacious space. But when they got up they thought they had only slept for a few hours or maybe a day. They had actually stayed asleep for two or maybe three hundred years. Then the men gave some money to one of them to buy some food. They asked the man to be cautious, else people get to know and force them to their way of worship. But when the man went out, the world had changed. The pagans ruled no more. Christians called the shots. People's dress, language and food had changed too. So this man struck them as odd. The shopkeeper gathered others around him. He was questioned. Through him, they found out about the other men in the cave. Many people were surprised to see these men live for 200 or 300 years. They were all safe.
The rest embraced their faith. The men of the cave
greeted them, and soon breathed their last.

Being Kind to Orphans

The Prophet who was himself born an orphan, emphasised kind treatment of the orphans He is reported to have said, 'The best house among the Muslims is the one which contains an orphan who is well treated. And the worst house is the one which has an orphan who is ill treated.' The Quran too talks of treating orphans with kindness.

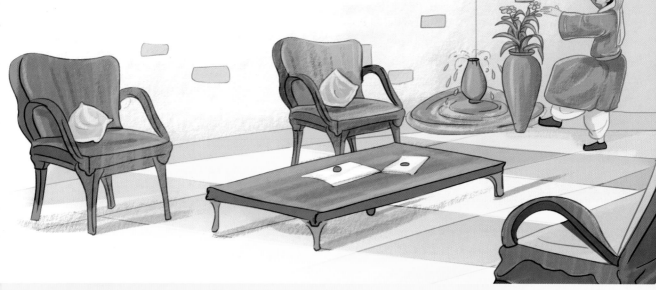

The Messenger

When the Prophet was intensely concerned about the welfare of the Quraish people who refused to believe him, there was a possibility that it might take a toll on his health. Allah told him that he was not to be blamed for others' errors or their refusal to believe the truth. The Prophet was told that his task was only to convey the message to people. He could invite them to the true path but guidance could only be provided by Allah. The failure of people to believe or to do good deeds cannot be blamed on him. The Prophet was to persevere with his mission, give good tidings to people who believe and warn them of the evil consequences of their not believing. But he was not to blame them for their shortcomings.

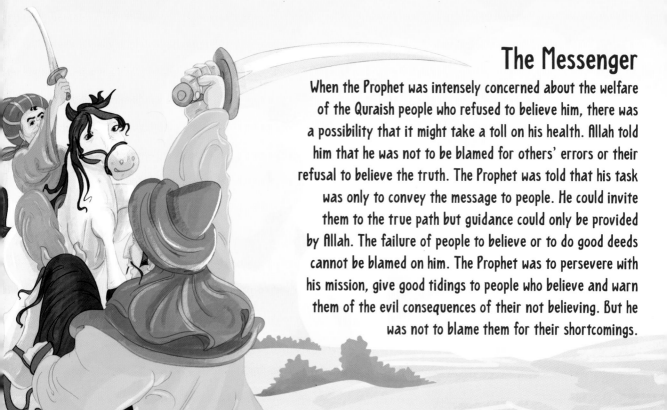

Building Mosques

Some Jews and Christians were in the habit of taking the graves of the prophets as places of worship. Allah cursed them. Cursed too, were those who built a place of worship over the grave when a pious person among them died. Hence the Prophet forbade building a mosque or any place of worship over a grave.

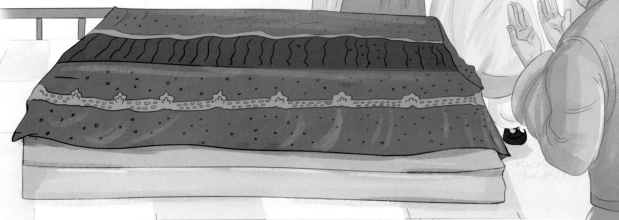

He is reported to have said, 'Lo! Those who preceded you made the graves of their prophets into places of worship but I forbid you from it.' He did not want anyone, including himself, to be deified. He wanted all focus to be on Allah.

Last Day

The Day of Resurrection, the time all dead are said to be brought alive and stand before Allah to give an account of their actions, is drawing near. The arrival of Prophet Muhammad marked the beginning of the last chapter in human history. The Prophet too was often asked about the Day of Resurrection or the Day of Judgment and how close or how far was it. The Prophet pointed to his two fingers and said, 'I and the Hour are (close to each other) like these two fingers.' Thus, it is even more important to do good deeds.

Standing Up for Justice

Once, a member of the Arash tribe came to Makkah with some camels. Abu Jahl bought the camels but dilly-dallied about the payment. The man from the Arash community went to ask for help from the Quraish chiefs who, however, pointed him to Prophet Muhammad who was at the time, sitting in a corner quietly. They wanted to see what would be his reaction. When the man conveyed his grievance to the Prophet, he immediately went to Abu Jahl.

People thought there would be a fight. But the Prophet simply told Abu Jahl to pay the man his due. Onlookers were surprised. They were expecting resistance. The personality of the Prophet and the power of his speech were too much to resist for Abu Jahl. Abu Jahl did accordingly.

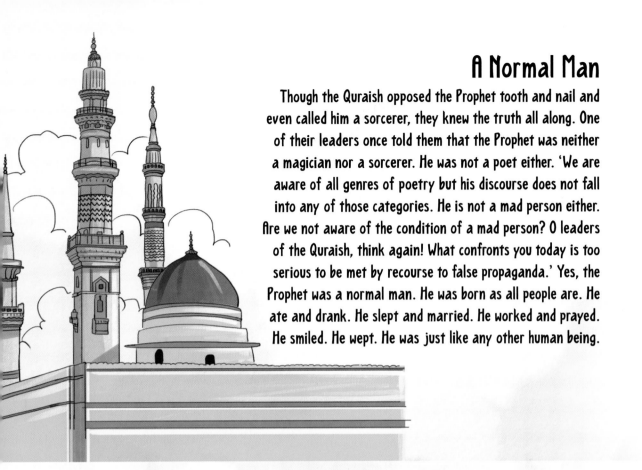

A Normal Man

Though the Quraish opposed the Prophet tooth and nail and even called him a sorcerer, they knew the truth all along. One of their leaders once told them that the Prophet was neither a magician nor a sorcerer. He was not a poet either. 'We are aware of all genres of poetry but his discourse does not fall into any of those categories. He is not a mad person either. Are we not aware of the condition of a mad person? O leaders of the Quraish, think again! What confronts you today is too serious to be met by recourse to false propaganda.' Yes, the Prophet was a normal man. He was born as all people are. He ate and drank. He slept and married. He worked and prayed. He smiled. He wept. He was just like any other human being.

Paradise and This World

Life in Paradise must have been beautiful for Adam. He was Allah's vice regent there and enjoyed the best of food, drinks and clothing. Angels were at his beck and call. He did not have to worry about day-to-day needs. His focus was on the higher demands of being the vice regent. Yet, Allah wanted to check Adam's mettle to see how fit he was for Paradise. So a test was devised. The result of the test proved that Adam was susceptible to temptation. He was forgetful too. Thus, he was given a probationary rather than permanent residency of Paradise. During this period of probation, Allah denied Adam some of the luxuries conferred upon him earlier. The luxuries and the privileges would await him in the Next Life for those who obey Allah and resist Shaitaan. Thus, this worldly life is the period of probation for all progeny of Adam.

Misleading Adam

The Quran tells us that it was Adam rather than Eve who was first misled by Shaitaan. Both of them together though, were misled by Shaitaan. Once they disobeyed Allah's command, they were gradually deprived of some of the privileges given to them earlier. They were first deprived of their clothing. Then the arrangements for food, water and shelter without any effort on their part, were also withdrawn. It was only when they were hungry that they realised the value of being satiated. The same happened with their understanding of clothing and shelter. Thus, when we face such trials, we understand our blessings.

Shaitaan

Shaitaan took a pledge to mislead Allah's creation. He decided to lie in wait for mankind to mislead the gullible. He openly warned Adam that he would try to mislead him. Such was his skill at taking people astray that he was able to mislead Adam with the promise of eternal life and an endless bliss. Shaitaan threw such temptations at Adam that he fell into his trap. However, Adam believed in Allah, realised his mistake and sought pardon from Allah. Thus, he was not banished from grace and was selected for special service to Allah.

Pray Whenever You Remember

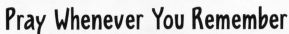

We pray five times a day. But what is the purpose of prayer? It is done so that we don't forget Allah, His bounties and His mercy. Prayer reminds us of our station in life. Such is the importance of five daily prayers that it is said that if one forgets to offer prayer at the appointed time, one should do so as soon as one remembers. The Prophet said, 'One who forgets to perform prayers should do so whenever he recalls it. Nothing else is required.'

Cleaning Dirt

The Prophet instructed people to clean their shoes before entering the prayer house. In case one stepped into filth, the Prophet said, 'When any of you comes to the mosque, he should have a look at his shoes and clean them by rubbing them against the earth if they are soiled with filth and offer prayers with your shoes on.' One can offer prayers, particularly the funeral prayers, with the shoes on, as long as they are clean of filth.

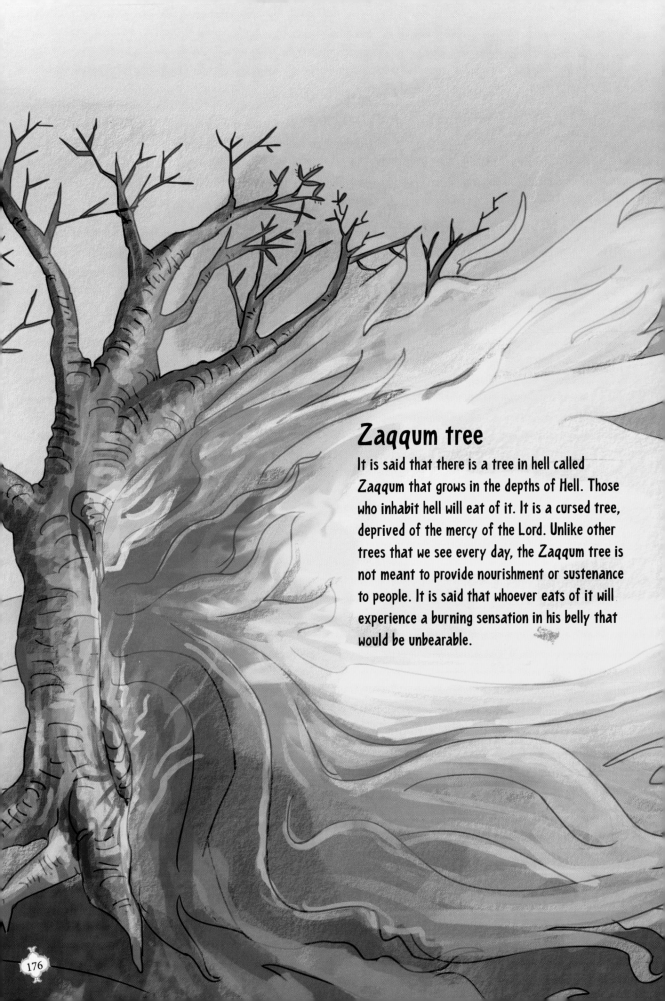

Zaqqum tree

It is said that there is a tree in hell called Zaqqum that grows in the depths of Hell. Those who inhabit hell will eat of it. It is a cursed tree, deprived of the mercy of the Lord. Unlike other trees that we see every day, the Zaqqum tree is not meant to provide nourishment or sustenance to people. It is said that whoever eats of it will experience a burning sensation in his belly that would be unbearable.

The Report Card

On the Day of Judgment, we will all be held to account for our deeds; the smallest of good deeds will be rewarded and there will be an account of the most minute of sins. It is said that those who will be handed over the scroll of their deeds in their right hand will rejoice to see the contents. Like little boys and girls, they will show it to others. Those who will be given their scroll in their left hand will be considered the evil-doers. They will hide their scroll behind their back, ashamed of their deeds.

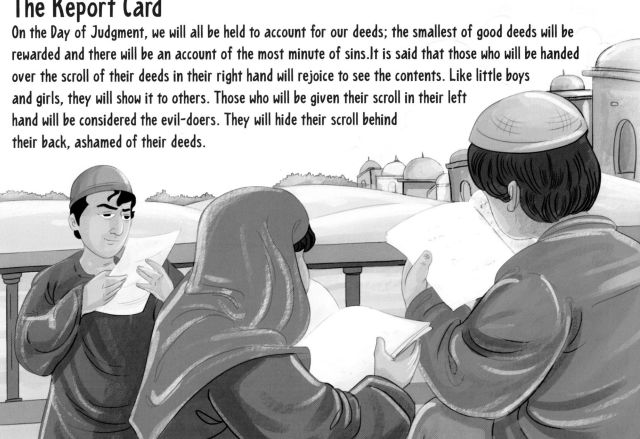

Controlling Anger

We can either master our emotions or let emotions master us. The strong man is not one with physical strength but one who has control over himself. Prophet Muhammad said, 'The strong one controls himself while in anger.' Anger is the root cause of many evils. The Shaitaan that may be inside us comes out in the form of anger. The Quran tells us to control anger to avoid the Shaitaan. It further goes on to say, 'And if an evil suggestion comes to you from Shaitaan, then seek refuge in Allah. He is hearing and knowing.' And how does one seek refuge with Allah? One can recite, 'Aauzu billahi mina shaitaan nir rajeem (I seek refuge in Allah from Shaitaan, the outcast).'

Allah Willing

Allah does not like it when we claim that we will do something without adding, 'In sha Allah (If Allah wills).' This is to help us avoid gloating in pride over our deeds. There is an incident revealed in the Quran that talks of a man who had a big orchard. He had a stream flowing through it and had plenty of date palms. He was proud of his wealth, and would boast to his neighbour that he was wealthier and stronger than him. He believed his riches would never perish. He would continue to enjoy all the luxuries of his

orchard. One night, a storm overtook his orchard, ruining everything. His neighbour corrected him, 'When you entered your orchard, why did you not say, 'Whatever Allah wills shall come to pass for there is no power greater than Allah!' Eventually, the produce of the rich man was fully destroyed and he ended up holding his head in despair, saying, 'Wish I had acknowledged my Lord in His divinity.' Whatever happens, happens with the will of Allah.

Cleanliness Is Essential

The Prophet wanted every individual to remain clean all the time. That is why, he stressed ablution before the five daily prayers and wearing clean clothes. A dirty piece of cloth could not be used for establishing prayer. He is reported to have said, 'Cleanliness is a part of the faith.'

Bilal and His Hopeful Actions

Bilal was the first man to give the athaan, the prayer call. It is related by Abu Hurairah that the Prophet said to Bilal, 'Tell me, Bilal, of your most hopeful action since your acceptance of Islam, for I have heard the echo of your footsteps in Paradise in front of me.' Bilal replied, 'I do not consider any of my actions more hopeful than that whenever I have performed my ablutions during the day or night, I have each time offered by way of prayer that which had been prescribed for me.'

اللهُ أَكْبَرُ ـ اللهُ أَكْبَرُ ـ اللهُ أَكْبَرُ ـ اللهُ أَكْبَرُ

أَشْهَدُ أَنْ لَا إِلَهَ إِلَّا اللهُ ـ أَشْهَدُ أَنْ لَا إِلَهَ إِلَّا اللهُ

أَشْهَدُ أَنَّ مُحَمَّدًا رَسُولُ اللهِ ـ أَشْهَدُ أَنَّ مُحَمَّدًا رَسُولُ اللهِ

حَيَّ عَلَى الصَّلَوةِ ـ حَيَّ عَلَى الصَّلَوةِ

حَيَّ عَلَى الْفَلَاحِ ـ حَيَّ عَلَى الْفَلَاحِ

اللهُ أَكْبَرُ ـ اللهُ أَكْبَرُ

لَا إِلَهَ إِلَّا اللهُ

Two Rakaat before Fajr Jamaat

Time for Fajr, the dawn prayer was drawing near. Bilal got ready to apprise the Prophet of the approaching time for prayer. Along the way, he met the Prophet's wife, Ayesha. He got busy with some other matter until he saw that the first light was fast approaching. He rose to inform the Prophet. The Prophet did not come out immediately. The Prophet offered two rakaat before coming out. He said, 'Messenger of Allah! You let the light spread.' The Prophet replied, 'Even if the light had spread more than it did, I would have offered two rakaat well and handsomely.'

Seeking Help with Patience

Once a man was in deep trouble. He had failed in his business. He had lost all his money and his property was gone too. He was depressed and reached out to an imam for help. The imam told him to read two verses of the Quran as often as he could. Those would give him peace and strength.

Pray, what were the two verses? They were the last verses of Surah Baqarah which ends with this prayer, 'Allah does not burden a soul beyond that it can bear.' The second verse he was asked to read advised him thus, 'And seek help in patience and prayers.' The verses told him that there was no burden for which God had not prepared him.

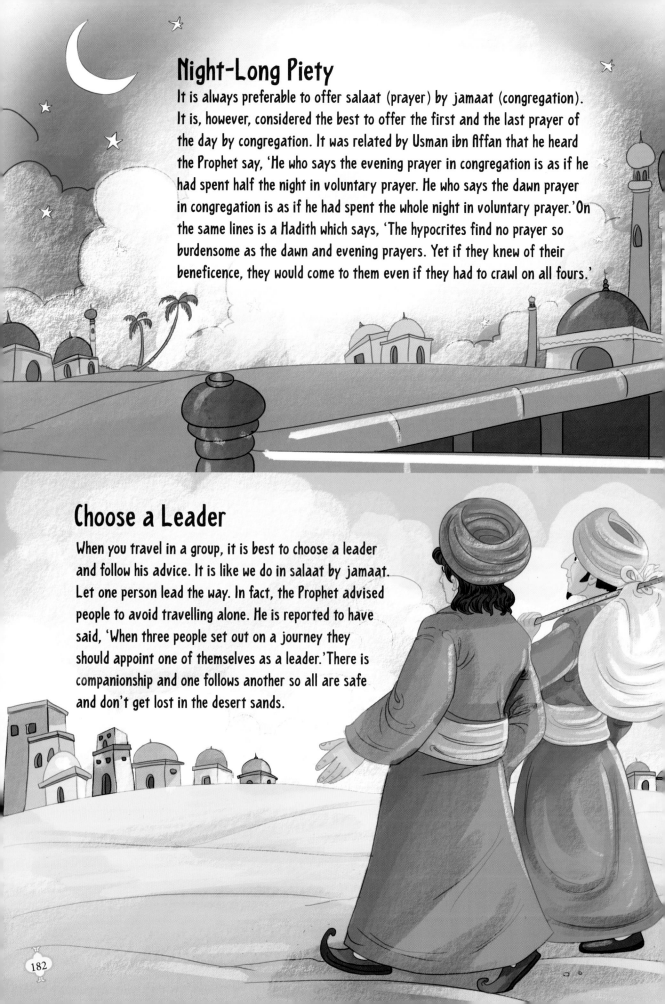

Night-Long Piety

It is always preferable to offer salaat (prayer) by jamaat (congregation). It is, however, considered the best to offer the first and the last prayer of the day by congregation. It was related by Usman ibn Affan that he heard the Prophet say, 'He who says the evening prayer in congregation is as if he had spent half the night in voluntary prayer. He who says the dawn prayer in congregation is as if he had spent the whole night in voluntary prayer.' On the same lines is a Hadith which says, 'The hypocrites find no prayer so burdensome as the dawn and evening prayers. Yet if they knew of their beneficence, they would come to them even if they had to crawl on all fours.'

Choose a Leader

When you travel in a group, it is best to choose a leader and follow his advice. It is like we do in salaat by jamaat. Let one person lead the way. In fact, the Prophet advised people to avoid travelling alone. He is reported to have said, 'When three people set out on a journey they should appoint one of themselves as a leader.' There is companionship and one follows another so all are safe and don't get lost in the desert sands.

Worker's Wages

The Quran tells us clearly, 'Fulfil your covenants for you will be called to account for your covenants.' The Prophet too was unambiguous about denouncing those who break their covenants. He is reported to have stated, 'Allah, the Exalted, says there are three against whom I shall contend on the Day of Judgment. One, he who makes a covenant in My name and then defaults on it; two, he who sells a free man into slavery and devours his price; and three, he who hires a workman and having taken full work from him, fails to pay him his wages.' That is why it has been made clear in Islam that the worker should be paid his due before the sweat on his body dries up.

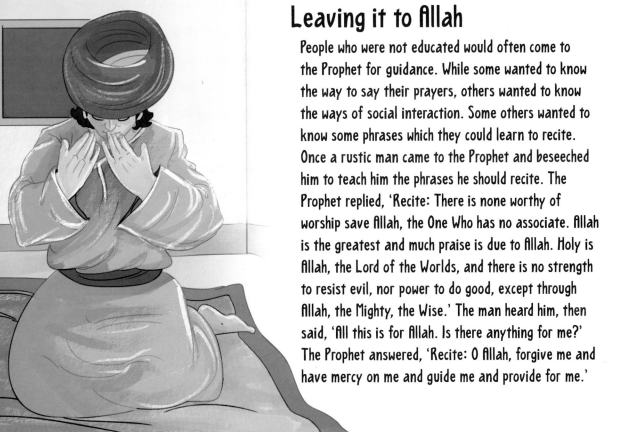

Leaving it to Allah

People who were not educated would often come to the Prophet for guidance. While some wanted to know the way to say their prayers, others wanted to know the ways of social interaction. Some others wanted to know some phrases which they could learn to recite. Once a rustic man came to the Prophet and beseeched him to teach him the phrases he should recite. The Prophet replied, 'Recite: There is none worthy of worship save Allah, the One Who has no associate. Allah is the greatest and much praise is due to Allah. Holy is Allah, the Lord of the Worlds, and there is no strength to resist evil, nor power to do good, except through Allah, the Mighty, the Wise.' The man heard him, then said, 'All this is for Allah. Is there anything for me?' The Prophet answered, 'Recite: O Allah, forgive me and have mercy on me and guide me and provide for me.'

Allah's Book

Once the Prophet was asked about what an ideal speech must be. He replied, 'The most accurate and truthful speech is the Book of Allah.' On another occasion, he said, 'The best of you is the one who learned and taught the Quran.' As he lived in an era when most people in that region were not educated, he added, 'The one who recites the Quran and the one who listens to it, have an equal reward.'

The Qaris

Once some people came to the Prophet and requested him to send some men with them who could teach them the Quran and the Sunnah. The Prophet sent seventy men with them from the Ansar tribe. They were known as qaris. These people would recite the Quran. At night, they would teach it. During the day, they brought water to the mosque, besides gathering firewood for fuel. They would sell it and with the proceeds they used to purchase food for those who remained behind in attendance in mosques, besides the needy. They were sent by the Prophet because people asked for them, but they were slaughtered on their way. Those who were slaughtered, prayed, 'O Allah, convey from us to our Prophet that we have reached You and are pleased with You and You are pleased with us.' When the Prophet got the news, he conveyed it to his brethren, and they supplicated, 'O Allah, convey from us to our Prophet that we have reached You and are pleased with You, and that You are pleased with us.'

Allah Forgives

Prophet Muhammad revealed that the Shaitaan said to Allah, 'I shall continue to lead your servants astray as long as their spirits are in their bodies.' Allah replied, 'I shall continue to pardon them as long as they ask for My forgiveness.' Allah forgives. Don't ever forget to ask for it.

Protect the Rights of Non-Muslims

Islam gives complete right to anybody to follow his or her own religion. Nobody can be harassed for following a particular religion. Prophet Muhammad maintained good relations with the Jews and the Christians in the land and never once asked a non-Muslim when he joined Islam about his actions of the past. Assuring non-Muslim minorities a life with dignity in Medina, he is reported to have said, 'Beware! Whoever is cruel or harsh to a non-Muslim minority, curtailing their rights, overburdening them or stealing from them, I will complain to Allah about that person on the Day of Judgment.'

Brothers to the Messenger

Once Prophet Muhammad expressed a desire to meet his brothers. His companions were surprised to hear that wish. They asked him, 'Are not we your brothers?' The Prophet replied, 'You are my companions.' Then who are the brothers of the last prophet of Islam? Well, the answer was given by the Prophet himself. He said, 'My brothers are those who will believe in me without having seen me.'

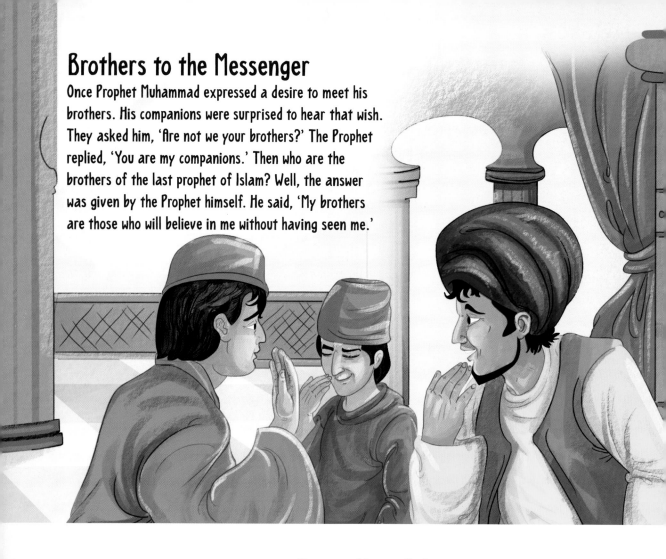

Being Merciful

In Islam, justice is appreciated, but mercy is considered even better. Prophet Muhammad said, 'Those who are merciful will be shown mercy by the Most Merciful. Be merciful to those on earth, and the One in the heaven will have mercy upon you.' He preached, 'Don't do evil to those who do evil to you but deal with them with forgiveness and kindness.'

Kisra's Bracelet

Once Prophet Muhammad told Suraqa, the man who chased him on his horse, that one day, he will wear the bracelet of Kisra and will be a powerful emperor of the Sassanid Empire. Suraqa laughed it off. When the Prophet told him that Kisra was the son of Hormuz, Suraqa went away, not quite believing a word of it all. The Prophet passed away after a few years of this incident. Suraqa had become one of the believers. Caliph Umar held the reins. The Muslim empire now included Persia from where great riches reached the caliph. Among the items of the booty was an expensive bracelet of Kisra!

Caliph Umar immediately called over Suraqa and gave him the bracelet. This surprised Suraqa and tears came to his eyes. This action fulfilled the word of the Prophet.

A Day of Fifty Thousand Years

The Day of Judgment will be one long day. It will seem unending. It will be as long as Fifty Thousand Years! Yet, it is called the Day of Judgment. Why? Simply because what we know to be a day is a measure of the earth; what will be a day then will be equal to fifty thousand earth years. The Quran reinstates it in verse, 'The angels and the Rooh move up to Him in a Day the measure of which is fifty thousand years.'

Changing Levels of Faith

The level of people's faith goes up and down. When one is in a mosque or attending a sermon, one feels positively pious and intends to continue in that state. Yet, when we go to the market, school or college, the level of faith goes down. It again goes up when we stand for prayer. It happens with all of us. It used to happen with the companions of the Prophet too. Once, a companion wondered if he was a hypocrite simply because when he was in the company of the Prophet or read the Quran, he felt spiritually elevated but the feeling went down when he got involved with everyday responsibilities. So he presented his case before the Prophet. The Prophet said, 'If you had the same feelings when you are here with me and when you are with your family or when you are at work, the angels in the street would want to shake hands with you. It will be because your level of imaan will be so high.' Then he added, 'Let's try an hour and an hour.' It meant we can put aside an hour a day for purification of the heart and an hour for our worldly pursuits. In other words, we must fulfil our duties to our family, neighbours, friends, colleagues and also fulfil our obligation towards Allah. Islam is all about striking a balance and it is okay to feel the ups and downs of life.

Barefoot

There will be a day when everybody will pass away. All men and women, boys and girls and all birds, animals and insects. That is the day on which all those who had tasted death will be brought before Allah. That will be the Day of Judgment. Everybody will be bareheaded and barefoot. Not a shirt on anybody's back, not a garment over their body. When the Prophet's wife Ayesha got to know this, she wondered if men and women will be together in that condition. And won't people look at each other? So she asked her husband about it. The Prophet told her, 'The situation will be more overwhelming than you can imagine, O Siddiq's daughter. The matter will be too serious for them to take notice. On that Day, people will look totally confused, even intoxicated. People will feel the heat. The sun will be very close to them. They will sweat a lot. Only some people will be in Allah's shade. They will be pious people and those who are obedient to Allah.' Also, there will be people who spend in charity.

Being under the Shade

On the Day of Judgment, as people will stand perspiring from head to foot, and not sure of the judgment that awaits them, there will be some people who will enjoy Allah's shade. They will be protected from the heat of the sun. They will be the people who would have done good deeds. The Prophet listed seven such types of people. According to him, 'There are seven types of people whom Allah will shade on the Day when there is no shade except His shade. They will be a fair ruler; a youth who grew up in the worship of Allah; a man whose heart is attached to the mosques; two people who love each other for Allah's sake; a man who is called by a woman of beauty, but he says, 'I fear Allah'; a man who gives in charity and hides it; and a person who remembered Allah in private, and so his eyes shed tears.'

Conversations with Allah

Often at the end of salaat in a mosque, people are requested to stay on for 'deen ki baat' (talk of faith). What people often do not realise is that the salaat itself is 'deen ki baat' or conversation with Allah. When we pray to Allah, we converse with Him. When we read the Quran, Allah converses with us.

At the beginning of every rakat, we recite Surah Fateha, the opening verse of the Quran. No prayer is complete without it. And Surah Fateha is the only surah of the Quran where we talk to Allah. In all other hundred and thirteen surahs, Allah talks to us. When we express His praises in Surah Fateha, He answers. When we say, 'You alone do we worship, your help alone do we seek,' He answers. So, next time you have a problem, a little sorrow, share it with Allah and talk to Him. Offer salaat and be certain He answers all calls.

سُوْرَةُ الفَاتِحَة

بِسْمِ اللهِ الرَّحْمٰنِ الرَّحِيْمِ
اَلْحَمْدُ لِلّٰهِ رَبِّ الْعٰلَمِيْنَ ۙ الرَّحْمٰنِ الرَّحِيْمِ ۙ
مٰلِكِ يَوْمِ الدِّيْنِ ۙ اِيَّاكَ نَعْبُدُ وَاِيَّاكَ نَسْتَعِيْنُ ۙ
اِهْدِنَا الصِّرَاطَ الْمُسْتَقِيْمَ ۙ صِرَاطَ الَّذِيْنَ اَنْعَمْتَ
عَلَيْهِمْ ۙ غَيْرِ الْمَغْضُوْبِ عَلَيْهِمْ وَلَا الضَّآلِّيْنَ

Striking a Balance

Allah wants us to be in this world as if we are taking an examination. That is, focus on the task ahead, answer the questions given and move on. Nobody stays on in an examination hall forever. There comes a time when we are given our result. It is the same way with this world. We will be given our result on the Day of Judgment. But before that, we have to live in this world. It is here that we have to strike a balance between deen (faith) and duniya (world). While we have to live here for the Hereafter, we have to fulfil our commitments to people around us, to the world and, to our family. We have to pursue our career, be the best doctor, cricketer or engineer that we can be. We also have to take out time to think and ponder about the purpose of our lives and why we are here and be the best human beings we can be.

Look the Best

Be the best you can be! Look the best you can. Wear the best available. Islam instructs people to wear good clothes when they go out to offer salaat. Men are to shun the use of onion and garlic just before going to mosque for fear of their odour putting off the man standing next to them in salaat. Use of perfumes like itar is encouraged. Once a companion of the Prophet revealed that he was fond of wearing nice clothes and good shoes. He wondered if he was guilty of arrogance. The Prophet said, 'No. Allah is beautiful and loves beauty.' The Prophet approved of wearing nice clothes, even fashionable clothes that cover our body. He disapproved of clothes that reveal our body, as clothes are meant to cover the body.

Value

A man used to bring things from his village to sell in the city of Madinah. Occasionally, he would bring small gifts for the Prophet. The Prophet too, would give him a return gift. He would call this man his friend. One day, this man stood in the market, selling goods. The Prophet saw him and decided to surprise him by going from behind and embracing him. The man was surprised and brashly asked the man to free him. Then he realised that the Prophet was hugging him. He did not want to walk away and wanted to remain in that position for some more time.

The Prophet was not done though. Laughingly, he said, 'Who will purchase this slave?' The man answered, 'You will be in a loss. No one will give you a good price.' The Prophet replied, 'No, even if people do not give you due respect, for Allah you are priceless.'

Grandfather's Lap

Prophet Muhammad laid emphasis on being gentle with children. He set an example for future generations to emulate with an incident while he was offering Isha-the concluding salaat of the day. His grandsons Hassan and Hussain were running around. The boys would get on their grandfather's back when he prayed. It was narrated by Abu Hurairah, 'We were praying Isha with the messenger of Allah. When he would prostrate, Hassan and Hussain would jump on his back. When he would rise, he would pick them up from his back and gently put them on the floor. When he went back to prostrating, they would again climb over him.' At the conclusion of the prayer, the Prophet would cheerfully take the little boys and make them sit on his lap.

The Yellow Dress

Many clerics tend to be uptight with children, not allowing them to disturb them when they pray or even when they meet their guests. The Prophet used to indulge children. Once, a girl came to him with her father. She was wearing a nice yellow dress in which she twirled and swayed in front of the Prophet as little children like to do. The Prophet liked her dress very much, and said, 'Sanah, sanah.' It meant, 'Nice, nice.' The girl was happy to receive a compliment for her dress. She started playing with the ring of the Prophet, whereupon her father stopped her. The Prophet did not mind and asked her father to let her continue to play. As she played, he gave her a blessing, 'Wear out and consume, wear out and consume.' It meant that she should have more and more garments to wear.

Keeping Promises

It is important to keep our promises. Prophet Muhammad used to insist that nobody was allowed to make a false promise to children merely because they were small. Once, he went to a companion's house. The companion's little boy, Abdullah ran around the Prophet, hugely enjoying the experience of having him over. Just then, the child's mother called for him. The boy did not respond. Then she called him again, promising to give him a date. The boy went. The mother was about to continue her work when the Prophet came in front of her. At this, the Prophet responded, 'If you do not intend to give him a date now, it will be recorded on you as a lie.' The woman realised her callousness and quickly brought out a date from a jar at the counter and gave it to the child waiting with twinkling eyes!

Children's Rights

Parents are expected to be courteous and polite even when correcting the faults of their children. The best gift for children, according to the Prophet, is education. The Prophet used to say, 'The best gift a father can give to his children is education.' He believed that each one was responsible and each one was accountable. He instructed humans not to kill children for fear of poverty. 'Allah will provide for them as He provides for you.'

Practice What You Preach

The Quran tells us to be grateful to Allah for all the blessings we enjoy. The Prophet himself never forgot a kind deed. He would always be grateful to anybody who helped him. Such was his personality that his enemies became his followers after meeting him. Yet, among the people he was grateful to, the first name had to be of his wife Khadijah. She comforted him and stood by him when the going got tough for the Prophet and his companions. The Prophet recalled, 'She believed in me when no one else did. She accepted Islam when people rejected me. She helped and comforted me when there was no one else to lend me a helping hand.' He never forgot that. What he preached, he followed in his life.

Literacy

Once upon a time, the Prophet and his companions had won their first war. It was the first time they had tasted success. The companions brought with them many prisoners of war. The prisoners of war were all non-Muslims. They had their own way of worship, their own way of life and their own culture. They wanted their freedom and their way of life back. The Prophet agreed. He, however, put a condition. Each prisoner had to teach ten children to read and write. Thus, he made each prisoner a teacher and the Muslim community which was in need of educated boys and girls, began to have members who would at least know how to read and write which the Prophet had not known as a child himself.

Helping a Man in Debt

It is considered our duty to visit the ailing, help the poor, even write off the money of a man in debt. The Prophet said, 'If anyone would like Allah to save him from the hardship of the Day of Resurrection, he should give more time to his debtor who is short of money or remit the debt altogether.' While even putting a morsel of food in the mouth of the wife is considered charity, to give something to a poor man brings one rewards as well. But giving the same to needy relations brings two rewards; one for charity, the other for respecting family ties.

The Undoing

In Islam, the wronged one is to be supported. The wrongdoer too is to be helped. During the time of the Prophet, some men were sitting. A man passed by, greeting them all. The men sitting there responded to his greeting. However, just as he moved away, one of them said, 'I hate this man!' A member of the group objected and threatened to tell this man. Upon this, he was told to do as he wished. So he went and told the man the truth. The man who had earlier greeted, now felt bad. He went to complain to the Prophet. He said, 'I passed by a group of Muslims. I greeted them. They returned my greeting. When I had left, one of them caught up with me and said that his fellow man hated me. Why? I am hurt! By Allah! Call him and ask him, why he hates me.' So the messenger of Allah called for this man and asked him the reason. He said, 'I am his neighbour and I know him very well. By Allah! I have never seen him pray any extra prayer except the prescribed prayer which everyone, good or bad alike, prays.' At this, the man who was so hated, interjected, saying, 'Ask him, O messenger of Allah! Has he ever seen me delaying my prayer, or not doing wudu properly, or not doing ruku (bowing position in prayer) or sujood properly?' The other man agreed he had never seen him do that, but added, 'By Allah! I have never seen him fast at all except this month which everyone, good or bad alike, fasts.'

The hurt man intervened, saying, 'O Messenger of Allah! Has he ever seen me breaking my fast during (the month) or doing anything to invalidate that fast?' The Prophet asked him, and he once again replied, 'No.' Once again he added, 'By Allah! I have never seen him giving to any needy person or spending any of his wealth for the sake of Allah, except for the mandatory zakaat which everyone, good or bad alike, gives.' At this, the man interjected yet again, saying, 'Ask him, O messenger of Allah! Have I ever withheld part of the zakaat or kept it back from the one who asked for it?' The other man again said, 'No.' Following this, the Prophet told the righteous Muslim, 'I don't know. Maybe, he is better than you.' The other man never made a pretence of what he did and did it sincerely. That was enough. The Prophet's wise words thus, silenced the indignant man.

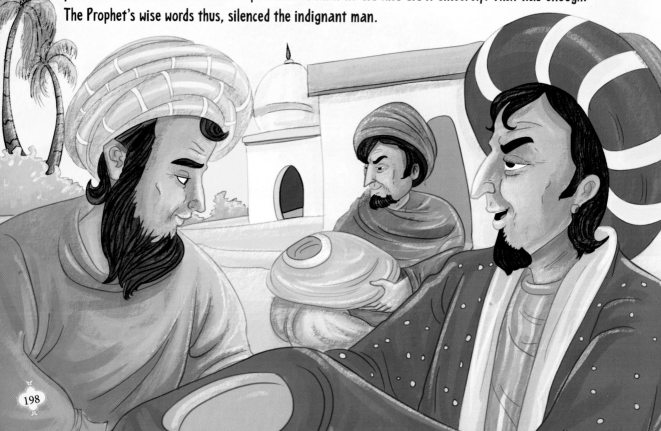

Flesh of the Brother

Forgive and forget, that is what they teach us in school. The Prophet too advised his companions on the same lines. It was narrated by Anas ibn Maalik, 'The Arabs used to serve one another while travelling and Abu Bakr and Umar had a man with them who was serving them. They fell asleep and then woke up. He had not prepared any food for them. One of them said to the other, 'This man sleeps too much.' They woke him. And told him to go to the messenger of Allah, and tell him, 'Abu Bakr and Umar send their salaams to you and are asking for food.' The Prophet said, 'Send my salaam to them and tell them they have already eaten.' They got worried and came to the Prophet, and said, 'O messenger of Allah! We sent word to you asking for food, and you told us we had already eaten. What have we eaten?' The Prophet said, 'The flesh of your brother. By the One in Whose hand is soul, I can see his flesh between your teeth.' At this they asked for forgiveness. The Prophet replied, 'Let him ask for forgiveness for you.' It meant that in Islam, a man who talks behind someone's back will not be pardoned until the man talked ill of him pardons him!

Many Faces of Charity

Zakaat is an obligatory form of charity while sadqa is voluntary charity. We can pay charity not just with money but even by merely smiling at a brother. The Prophet said, 'Your smile for your brother is charity. Your removal of stones from the people's path is charity. Your guidance of a person who is lost is charity.' Thus something as simple as giving directions to a person looking for an address is a form of charity. The Prophet used to say, 'A charity is due for every joint in each person on every day the sun comes up; to act justly between two people is a charity; to help a man with his mount; lifting him onto it or hoisting up his belongings on it, is a charity. In other words, such simple things like helping an old man cross a road come under the acts of charity that will protect us on the Day of Judgment.'

As the Prophet said, 'The believer's shade on the Day of Judgment, will be his charity.' In this life, charity is said to stand between a person and calamity.

Being Sensitive to Other Beings

Children are often amused to see the mother birds with their little ones. They are even curious to pick the little ones and see just how they flutter their wings, how they eat and how they fly. The Prophet forbade us from harming or playing with life. It was narrated by one of the companions of the Prophet, 'We were on a journey and during the Prophet's absence, we saw a bird with its two chicks; we took them in our hands. The mother bird was circling above us in the air, beating its wings in grief at being parted from her children. When Prophet Muhammad returned, he said, 'Who has hurt the feelings of this bird by taking its chicks? Return them to her.'

Neighbours First

As a little boy, Hasan would get up in the wee hours to watch his mother, Fatimah, pray. He would in fact join her in Tahajjud prayers. Every night, Fatimah would pray for all men and women, seek forgiveness for their sins, and pray for Allah's grace for them. She did not forget any neighbour in her prayer. She never asked for anything for herself. One day, Hasan asked her at the conclusion of her prayer. 'Mother, you pray for all every day. Not a word for yourself or any one in the family. Why?'

The mother replied, 'O Hasan, remember, one thing: Neighbours first, and then the house.'

In Every Hardship there Is Relief

When we encounter setbacks in life, we take recourse to management books for positive thinking. We are often advised to read Feel Good books. What we forget is that the Quran is the greatest book for positive energy. All through its 114 surahs are guidelines for times good or bad. The Prophet often advised his companions to read the Quran for calm and peace. His advice was based on a true understanding of the book. For instance, the concluding verse of Surah Rum advises us to be patient in the face of adversity. It says, 'So be patient, Allah's promise is true.' Then there are messages of better days ahead with Surah Talaq, verse 4 telling us, 'And for those who fear Allah, He will make their path easy.' Similarly, there are words of solace for anybody facing defeat. They come clearly from Surah Sharah, verse 5-6, 'So verily with the hardship there is relief, verily with the hardship there is relief.'

Changes in Society

It took around ten years after Hijrah for Prophet Muhammad to bring about social change. During the period of transition people continued to take wine, (the Prophet himself never tasted it) did business according to the earlier set of rules and inherited property according to local customs. Some also engaged in short-term marriages called mutah. These principles were not in conformity with the Quran. Islamic law did not govern society in the desert lands at the time. All these things came to an end with the complete revelation of the Quran when Allah declared, 'Today, I have perfected for you your religion.' This was said in Surah Maidah. The same surah prohibited intoxicants, gambling, and instructed people to be true to their word.

Islamic Banking

The Quran makes trade legal but prohibits dealing in interest. When the injunctions about interest were revealed to Prophet Muhammad, people were allowed to keep whatever they had earned in the past but were told not to charge a single penny from thereon. Surah Baqarah expressly prohibits asking for interest or giving it. Those who insist on trading in interest are said to be at war with the Almighty and His Messenger. Verses two seventy-eight and two seventy-nine say, 'Believers, have fear of Allah, and give up what is still due to you from usury, if you are true believers. For, if you do not do so, then know that you are at war with Allah and His messenger.'

It is for this reason that Islamic banking came about in the modern world.

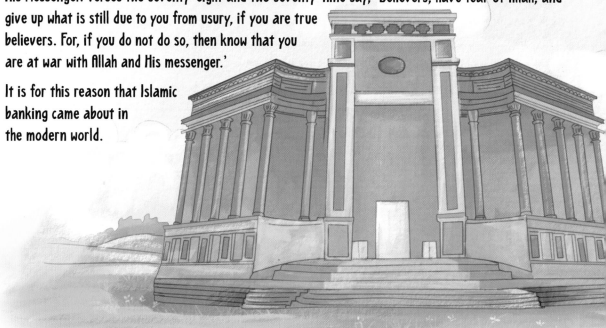

One Part Mercy

Allah is the most merciful. He not only has mercy on His creation, He also likes those who are kind and merciful. Allah divided mercy into a hundred parts. Of this He retained ninety-nine parts to Himself. He sent down to earth one part. It is because of this one part that people are kind to each other. Not just human beings but even animals show kindness to others. For instance, observe an adult animal with its baby and watch how the animal moves away from the body of the young one to avoid hurting it.

On the Day of Judgment we will all gain from this beautiful virtue.

Life in Paradise

We all seek Paradise. We are told to do good, shun evil to enter Paradise. Occasionally though, we wonder what will life be like in Paradise, for how long will we stay there and would we ever get tired of all the riches? For how long would we enjoy the overflowing rivers of milk and eat from countless platters of succulent grapes, dates, olives and pomegranates? Would we ever fall and hurt ourselves there and would there be doctors to attend to us? Our queries and doubts were answered by the Prophet who said, 'It will be said to the people of Paradise: You will now remain healthy forever and will never fall sick. You will live forever and never die. You will always remain young and never grow old. You will always remain settled and will never require to undertake the strain of a journey.' The inmates of Paradise will never need to toil for their daily bread. In case we are separated from our parents in Paradise, the children's prayer to Allah for their parents will enable the parents to meet us there. Unto Him shall we all return. Life is a journey from Him to Him.

Rizq

We are told again and again that Allah provides for us all. He gives the rizq (sustenance). The Quran makes it everybody's duty to invite people to Islam through Surah Nahl and Surah Qasas. People though often forget about extending an invitation and consider the word 'rizq' in the narrow sense of food or eatables. In Arabic though, the word 'rizq' is not confined to merely food. It covers all bounties of Allah, all things we take for granted, even the strength to follow the right path. We are told through tradition that when the baby rests in his mother's tummy, an angel comes down and writes down the baby's rizq. This rizq does not include only the food, the number of bites he or she is likely to have in a lifetime but also the deeds. Rizq includes all the mercies of Allah, including our knowledge, our ability to distinguish between right and wrong, good and bad, etc.

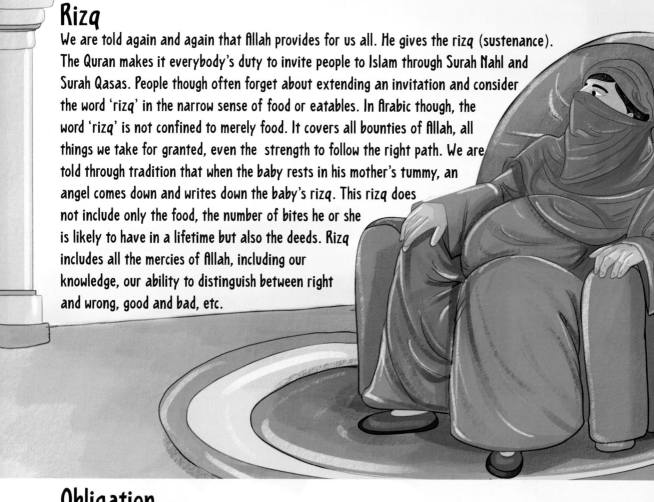

Obligation

It is important that we speak well of people or otherwise, stay quiet. Once upon a time, some companions of the Prophet happened to pass by a funeral. They praised the person who had passed away. The Prophet heard the praises for the deceased from his companions and remarked, 'It has become incumbent.' Then the companions happened to see another funeral. This time they did not say good things about the person who had passed away. Again, the Prophet heard their conversation and remarked, 'It has become incumbent.' His companions then asked him, 'What has become incumbent?' The Prophet replied, 'The one you praised, Paradise became incumbent upon him. For the other you spoke ill of, the Fire became incumbent for him. You are the witnesses of Allah upon the earth.'

Women and the Hereafter

Losing our loved ones is difficult. It is even more difficult if the parents lose their babies. Once a woman approached the Prophet, saying, 'O Messenger of Allah, the men relate that which they hear from you. Then appoint for us also a day when we could come to you to learn from you that which Allah has taught you.' The Prophet asked the woman to gather with other women on a particular day. The women gathered at the appointed time and date. Then the Prophet told them, 'Any of you who loses three children will be shielded from the Fire.' One of the women asked, 'And if there be two?' The Prophet replied, 'Even if there should be two.'

On another occasion, the Prophet told the faithful about the importance of girls in their lives. The Prophet held up his two fingers closely together and told those around him, 'He who has three daughters, and provides them good education, not differentiating between boys and girls, shall enter Paradise. On the Day of Judgment, he will be as close to me as these two fingers.' When a man wanted to know what would be the case if there were two girls, he gave the same answer. When a man asked about one girl, the Prophet repeated his response. Thus, women and girls play an important part in the journey to Paradise.

Charity that Multiplies

It is said that when a person breathes his last, his
account book draws to a close. His positive deeds of
public interest done in his lifetime keep adding up. For
instance, if the person got a well dug for the common people to drink from, he continues to be
rewarded as long as the well exists. Similarly, if one plants a tree and people take shade under it,
the person gets rewarded even after death. Similarly, providing education to the needy is an act of
sadqa jariah or charity that continues.

On the same lines are good, obedient children. If somebody leaves behind able and pious children,
their parents are rewarded for their good deeds. It was narrated by Abu Hurairah that the Prophet
said, 'When a person dies, his actions come to an end except in respect of three matters
that he leaves behind: a continuing charity, knowledge from which benefit for others
could be derived and righteous issue who pray for him.'

Ayesha, the wife of the Prophet, related something similar. According to her, a man
said to the Prophet, 'My mother has died suddenly. I believe if she could
have spoken she would have given away something in charity. Would it
count as meritorious on her part if I were to give away something in
charity on her behalf?' The Prophet thoughtfully confirmed. Any
deed of continuous charity is always valued.

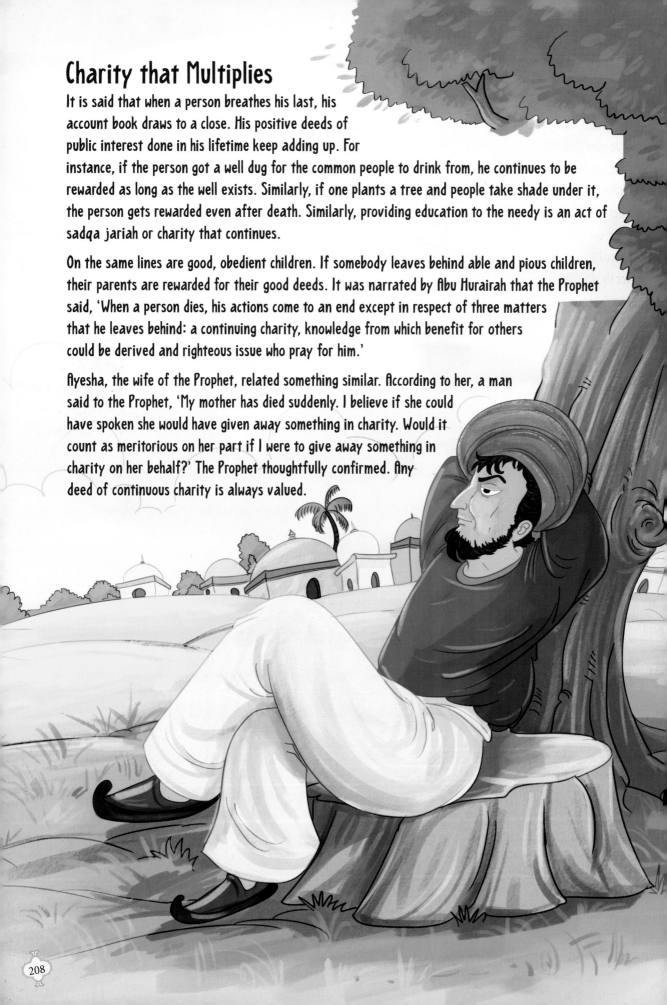

Time for Goodbyes

According to Ibn Shamasah, 'We were present with Amr Ibn As when he was in extremity. He wept for a long time and turned his face towards the wall. His son tried to comfort him, saying, 'Did not the Prophet give you good news? Did he not give you that good news?' Then the son turned his face towards us, and said, 'Our best preparation is the affirmation: There is none worthy of worship except Allah, and Muhammad is His messenger.' I have passed through three stages. I recall when no one was a more bitter enemy of the Prophet than myself; and if I had the power I would have put an end to him. Had I died in that condition, I would have been one of the denizens of the Fire. When Allah put Islam in my heart, I went to the Prophet and said, 'Extend your right hand, so that I might swear allegiance to you.' He put forth his right hand, but I withdrew my hand. He asked what was the matter. I said, 'I wish to make a condition. That my sins will be forgiven.' He said, 'Know that Islam wipes out all that has gone before it. Migration wipes out all that has gone before it and the Pilgrimage wipes out all that has gone before it.' Thereafter, no one was dearer to me than the Prophet, nor was anyone more glorious than him in my eyes. So bright was his glory that I could not look at his face for any length of time. Had I died in that condition, I could have hoped to be one of the dwellers of Paradise. Thereafter, we were made responsible for many things, and I do not know how I would fare with respect to them. When I die, no mourner should do so over my bier. When you bury me, throw the earth gently over me and tarry over my tomb for the space of time it takes to slaughter a camel and distribute its meat, so that I should draw comfort from your presence and can consider what answer I make to the messengers of my Lord.'

Walk to Salaat

When the muezzin gives calls for prayer with the athaan, leave everything and perform wudu or ablution. Get ready in clothes and depart. However, if the prayer is about to start any moment, exercise restraint, walk and do not run.

It was related by Abu Hurairah that he heard the Prophet say, 'When the Prayer service is about to commence, do not come running to it. Come to it walking calmly. Then join the service at the stage of your arrival, and make up afterward what you might have missed. For when one of you makes up his mind to join the salaat, he is already in salaat.'

The Long and Short of It

No sermon should go on for a long time and should never test the patience of people. It was related by Shaqiq Ibn Salamah, 'Ibn Masud used to preach every Thursday. A man said to him, 'Abu Abdur Rahman, I wish you would preach to us every day.' He said, 'What stops me from doing it is the fear lest I should bore you. I adopt the same method in preaching to you that the Prophet adopted in preaching to us out of fear of boring us.' Indeed, the Prophet had said, 'The length of a person's prayer and the brevity of his sermons testify to his intelligence. Make your prayers long and your sermons short.'

One Hand and Another

We are told in the Quran, 'That was why we laid it down for the Children of Israel that whoever killed a human being – except as punishment for murder or for spreading corruption in the land – shall be regarded as having killed all mankind, and whoever saved a human life shall be regarded as having saved all mankind.' There is a Hadith on the same lines that tells us to always refrain from killing one another. It was narrated by Abu Musa Ashari that the Prophet said, 'The relationship between one believer and another is like that between different parts of a building, one part strengthens the other.' Then he gripped the fingers of one hand between those of the other by way of illustration.

Good Word Is Charity

Allah wants us to be kind. He appreciates
gentleness. And reminds us in the Quran to be
gentle, polite and gracious. The Prophet too, wanted his followers to be
both kind and cheerful. He wanted them to be generous and charitable.
Adiyy Ibn Hatim related that the Prophet said, 'Shield yourselves
against the Fire even if it be only with half a date given in alms and
one who cannot afford even that much, should at least utter a good
word.' Thus, a good word becomes charity.

Be the Example

The best way to preach is to lead by example. However, if we only ask people to do good, be righteous, stay away from Shaitaan while we do not implement it ourselves, we would be guilty of hypocrisy and be a candidate for Hell. The Prophet used to say, 'A man will be brought on the Day of Judgment and will be thrown into the Fire. The denizens of the Fire will gather round him and say, 'What is this?

Did you not enjoin good and forbid evil?' He will say, 'That is so. I enjoined good but did not do it and I forbade evil but did it.'

The Quran too preaches through verse 104, Surah al-'Imran, 'Let there be a group among you who call others to do good and enjoin what is right, and forbid what is wrong. Those who do this shall be successful.'

The Witness

He was the last of the prophets of Islam, the last of the messengers. Earlier revealed books had prepared the prophets and their people for the coming of Muhammad. It is said in the Quran, 'When Allah made a covenant with the prophets, He said, 'Here is the book and the wisdom which I have given you. When there comes to you a messenger fulfilling that (predictions about him in their scripture) which is with you, you must believe in him and help him. Do you then affirm this and accept the responsibility I have laid upon you in these terms?' They said, 'We will affirm it.' Allah said, 'Then bear witness and I bear witness with you.'' Thus, man stands witness to the coming of the Prophet.

A Grain of Faith

Every Prophet who has set foot here had some disciples. Some, only a single one. Some only two. All of them faced opposition from the people and their prevalent beliefs. At times, people were guilty of dereliction of responsibility in the name of the

prophets. Prophet Muhammad said, 'Every one of the prophets raised before me had devoted disciples and companions who followed his practice and obeyed his directions. These were followed by those who said that which they did not do and did that which they were not commanded. He who challenges them with his hands is also a believer and he who challenges them with his tongue also is, as is he who challenges them with his heart. Beyond this there is not a grain of faith.'

He Who Disobeys....

We all want to enter Paradise. But how? The Prophet made the route simple for us. He said, 'All my people will enter Paradise, except those who deny.' He was asked, 'Who will be the deniers?' At this the Messenger of Allah said, 'He who obeys me will enter Paradise and he who disobeys me denies me.'

Walk to the Mosque

We are often driven down to the mosque for prayer even if the mosque is close by and we have time on our hands. It is, however, better to walk. For every step we take, an act of piety is written down under our name. During the time of the Prophet, there was a person whose house was the farthest from mosque. Yet he never missed a single salaat by jamaat. A man said to him, 'Why do you not purchase a donkey that you could ride in the dark and in the heat?' He refused as he preferred to walk to the mosque. Another suggested that he should buy a house close to the place of worship. He said, 'I would not like that my residence should be close to the mosque. I desire that my walking to the mosque and my return home from there should be recorded to my credit.' The Prophet said to him, 'Allah has credited all that to your account.' Indeed, all that you do with a good motive is credited to you.

Footprints

There was a companion of the Prophet who wanted to shift his residence closer to the mosque. He was, however, advised against it by the Prophet. The companion was Bani Salimah. When the Prophet got to know of the plan, he said, 'I have heard that you intend to move closer to the mosque.' Bani Salimah said, 'That is so, O Messenger of Allah, we intend to do that.' He said, 'Bani Salimah, keep to your homes, your footprints are recorded.'

The First Athaan

In the early days of the Prophet's life in Makkah, there were only a few Muslims. So they would gather easily for jamaat. After about a year of arrival in Makkah, it became more difficult as more people embraced the faith. Some stayed or worked far from the only masjid, Masjid ul Nabvi. So the Prophet looked for ways to inform people of the time for prayer. There were no watches then. A companion suggested that a bell could be rung before the prayer to call the people over. The idea was dropped as the Christians were already doing it. Another man suggested blowing a horn. It too was rejected as it was a Jewish practice. The Muslims needed something unique, something to call their own. Some other ideas were shared. A man suggested lighting a fire at the top of the hill so that people could see it. The Prophet rejected it. Another gave an

idea to raise a flag. It was not accepted. Just then Abdullah ibn Zaid shared a dream with everybody present. In that dream somebody taught him a way to call people for prayer. He was told to say, 'Allah-u-akbar, Allah-u-akbar, ashaduAllah illaha illalah....' The Prophet agreed with the beautiful dream and immediately called Bilal, a freed slave, to teach him the meanings of the sentences. Once he had learned the words, the Prophet asked him to go to a height and invite people over for prayer by pronouncing these words, loudly and clearly. Thus, came about the first athaan.

Reward of Athaan

The daily Athaan invites people to come and converse with the Lord. The invitation is not limited to men. Women too are invited. In fact, athaan throws open the doors of a masjid to whosoever believes in Allah and regards Prophet Muhammad to be His messenger. It includes not just men, but even jinn, insects, animals and other creatures.

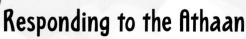

There is a Hadith wherein Abdullah bin Abdur Rahman reported that Abu Sa'id Al-Khudri said to me, 'I see that you are living among your sheep or in the wilderness, and you want to call athaan. You should raise your voice because whoever hears the athaan, whether a human or jinn or any other creature, will testify for you on the Day of Resurrection.' He had heard it from the Messenger of Allah. When the athaan is pronounced, the Shaitaan takes to his heels and does not return until the athaan is over.

Responding to the Athaan

Just as there are ample rewards for pronouncing the athaan, there are rules and benefits for listening to it with attention and responding to each sentence in an appropriate manner. When you hear the call for prayer, leave every activity and take to complete silence. The best way is to repeat after the muezzin the sentence he pronounces. When he says, 'Allah-u-akbar', you can repeat it. The same goes for the following two sentences. When he asks the people 'Come for prayer, come for success,' you must say 'La hawla wala quwwata ill billah (There is no might or power except in Allah).' Once the Athaan is over, one should ask Allah to exalt one's mention and place a request for an exalted status in Jannah.

Optional Fasting

Fasting is a must in the month of Ramadan, except for the old, ailing and the ones travelling. In fact, for this reason Ramadan is called the month of fasting. There is great spiritual and physical benefit in fasting for the thirty days in Ramadan. According to a Hadith, one does not know the exact reward of a fast. It is said, 'Every good deed of the son of Adam would be multiplied, a good deed receiving tenfold to seven hundred fold reward; Allah, the Exalted and Majestic has said, With the exception of fasting. For it is done for Me and I will give a reward for it, for one abandons his passion and food for My sake.'

There are optional fasts too. The Prophet himself used to fast every Monday and Thursday besides three days of the lunar calendar, the dates being 13, 14 and 15. Once he was asked by one of his companions, the reason for fasting every Monday and Thursday, the Prophet is reported to have said, 'The doors of Paradise open on Mondays and Thursdays and every servant of Allah who does not associate anything with Allah will be forgiven, except a man who has enmity and disputes with his Muslim brothers. In such a case, Allah would tell them to first reconcile their differences.'

The Suhoor Meal

Every fast begins with the pre-dawn meal called sehri or a suhoor meal. Many people tend to skip it, preferring to have a late dinner and going to bed rather than getting up in the wee hours to have a small meal. However, the Prophet did not approve of starting the fast in such a manner. He used to encourage his companions to have this meal. It was narrated by Anas ibn Maalik that Prophet Muhammad said, 'Eat suhoor, for in suhoor there is blessing.' The Prophet is said to have stated, 'Suhoor is a blessed meal. Do not omit it, even if one of you only takes a sip of water, for Allah and His angels send blessings on those who eat suhoor.' The Prophet regarded dates as the best meal for suhoor for they gave one the strength to face a long day ahead.

Fasting Joys

Fasting in Ramadan is compulsory, a farz. However, there is a sunnah or the way of the Prophet when it comes to breaking the fast. Fast or roza, or saum is broken with the setting of the sun or the call for maghrib prayer. At the time of breaking the fast, one must make a dua or a supplication. Any dua at this time is accepted. The supplication in Arabic is 'Allahumma laka sumtu wa'alaa rizqika aftartu (O Allah, I have fasted for You, believed in You, placed my trust in you and broken my fast on your provision).'

The Prophet used to break the fast with three dates. If dates were not available then he used to take water. He would say that whoever fasts, experiences two joys. He is joyful when he breaks his fast and is joyful because of his fasting when he meets his Lord.

Laylatul Qadr

Imagine being rewarded for the work of eighty-three years if you only put in a day's work! Or imagine, staying awake to pray for just one night and being rewarded as if you have done it for eighty-three years! Well, such are the returns of Laylatul Qadr, a night better than any in a year; a night that falls on any of the last ten days of Ramadan. Allah has promised His believers a great deal. They could earn the reward of regular prayers for a thousand months by praying with sincerity and honesty for this one night. A thousand months add up to around eighty-three years! The prayer can be a small personal one in place of the more frequently performed Tahajjud, or just reciting the Quran and making the supplication.

Laylatul Qadr is the night of prayer, night of power and the greatest night of the year, according to Islam. It is a special night because the Quran was sent down on this very night. It is the night when the angels descend down from the heavens.

Itikaf

Every act of piety carries manifold rewards in the month of Ramadan. The culmination of these acts comes with itikaf in the last ashra, the last ten days of the month. In itikaf, a person retreats to a local mosque, spending his time in peace and devotion without any worldly disturbance. In itikaf, a person spends most of his time in salaat, reciting the Quran, sacrificing his sleep. The Prophet used to perform itikaf for ten days every Ramadan, except the last Ramadan in his life when he doubled the days to twenty. There is great reward for performing itikaf. It is said that he who does so obtains the reward of two Hajj and two Umrahs – the compulsory and voluntary pilgrimage taken by Muslims, respectively. A person doing so is considered safe from sin and Hell.

Night of the New Moon

The Islamic calendar is a lunar calendar. Each new month starts with the arrival of the new moon. But no new month is anticipated with such eagerness as the arrival of the new moon for shawal. The first day of shawal marks Eid ul Fitr, the day which falls after thirty days of fasting in the month of Ramadan. Also called 'Meethi Eid' due to siwaiyan (a dessert consisting of milk, sugar and semolina) made on this day. It is considered a reward for a month of restraint and rigorous self-discipline.

On this day, special prayers are offered in the morning. This prayer is unlike any other prayer. It has two rakaat (cycles) with six takbir (calls) wherein the faithful stand and raise their hands to the ear and bring them down. It distinguishes it from the daily prayer. Also, a little money or food items are given to the poor as fitra. This is compulsory for every member of the family, from a one-day-old baby to a 100-year-old man. For babies and children, their parents give fitra before the Eid salaat. After salaat, people hug each other and exchange greetings. Of course, children are wealthier by the end of the day as they get their Eidi (a gift of abundance in the form of money) from the elders!

Titles of Each Surah

The surahs of the Quran, one hundred and fourteen in number, have been named to distinguish them from each other. The name of any surah does not mean that the surah contains material about that prophet, his personality, food item or even animal. For instance, the longest surah is called 'Baqarah' or Heifer/Calf. It contains information about the way of living, good and successful people, those gone astray, etc. It even talks of riba or interest. The surah concludes with the message that Allah does not lay on us a burden greater than we have a capacity to bear. None of it has any connection with a calf or heifer.

Similar is the case for the surahs, Surah Anam (Cattle) and Surah Raad (Thunder). The surahs named after various prophets like Hud, Yunus or Ibrahim have information or events related to them and also include information on other prophets. Interestingly, there is no surah named after Musa but he is mentioned more frequently than any other prophet in Islam in the book. Likewise, there are no surahs named after salaat or zakaat or sawm (fasting in the month of Ramadan, one of the pillars of Islam). Even Ramadan, the month in which the Quran was revealed, does not have a surah named after it. The absence of a surah named after it does not in any way take away the sanctity of Ramadan. Interestingly, there is a surah named after Prophet Muhammad, the messenger to whom the Quran was revealed!

Equality of Women

We all know about people killing the girl child. It is a horrible practice which has existed in many societies for centuries. There have been instances where little baby girls have been killed or buried alive for no fault of theirs except the fact that they were girls. Some were killed because of extreme poverty too. It was no different when Prophet Muhammad was born in Arabia. Many babies were killed only because they were female. But Prophet Muhammad spoke against all evil practices. He supported women in their rights to live freely, to seek education, to worship, to marry, to earn money and to inherit property. The Quran prohibits infanticide, male or female in clear terms. Surah Anam, verse 151 expresses it as, 'Say, Come! I will tell you what your Lord had really forbidden you! Do not associate anything

with Him; be good to your parents; and do not kill your children for fear of poverty – We shall provide sustenance for you as well as for them....'

The Hajj and Zamzam

Every Muslim wants to visit the Kaaba for Hajj. People make small savings to undertake the journey some day. Every year, an estimated 2.5 to 3 million people gather for Hajj from different parts of the world. But how did it start? The story goes back around four thousand years. Prophet Ibrahim's little son Ismail was very thirsty. They, along with Hajra, were stranded in the desert. Wherever they looked, the desert sands stretched as far as the eye could see. There was not a drop of water to drink. Hajra ran between the hills of Safa and Marwa to get some water for her son. Then she was ordered by Allah to hit the ground below her with her heel. Lo! A spring gushed forth. Ismail's thirst was quenched. It created a spring which to this day runs endlessly, giving the world 'Zamzam' the water said to carry great healing qualities. Today, when the pilgrims progress between Safa and Marwa, they do so quickly in a bid to recreate Hajra's run.

Women in the Mosque

Once a woman heard that we get twenty-seven times the reward for a single prayer in a congregation, at a mosque. She too wanted to join but she had a little baby. It was difficult for her. She had to look after household chores too. So she approached the Prophet, who said, 'If a lady prays at her home, it is better than the mosque – it is preferable for her to pray in the room.' Nowhere does the Quran prevent women from going to the mosque to offer prayer by jamaat if they choose to do so. They are to have their own saff (row), just as men are to have their own saff, with no intermingling of the genders taking place. The Prophet told the husbands at that time not to prevent their wives if they wanted to go to the mosque. There is another Hadith which says, 'Prevent not the servants of Allah who are females, from entering the mosques.' The Prophet is reported to have said that the best prayer for a man is in the first row of the congregation and the best prayer for a woman is in the last row. For Eid too, he was in favour of women proceeding to the mosque for prayer in new clothes, at least a new covering to wear over their old clothes. For those who could not afford a new covering, he asked them to wash it beforehand. He was also known to recite smaller surahs of the Quran in congregational prayer, keeping in mind little children who would be accompanied by their mothers. So women as well as men are part of the jamaat.

Making of the Kaaba

There is a rich history behind the building of the Kaaba. It is said that the the house of Allah was ordered to be constructed in the shape of the house of Heaven. Adam was the first to build it. It was destroyed during the flood, at the time of Nooh. It was Ibrahim who was ordained to build it afresh. The Quran clearly states, (Surah Baqarah, verse 125), 'And (remember) when We made the House (Kaaba), a place of assembly for men, and a house of safety; And you take the House of Ibrahim as a place of prayer; And We took the promise from Ibrahim and Ismail that they should cleanse My House for those who circle it round, or use it as a retreat, or bow, or prostrate themselves (in prayer).'

The Kaaba Ibrahim purified is the site around which the faithful take seven rounds (tawaf) during Hajj. A little before he passed away in 632 CE, Prophet Muhammad led his followers on a Hajj pilgrimage here, the only Hajj he ever performed. In Hajj, Muslims circumambulate the Kaaba. The path that the Prophet travelled for Hajj is retraced to this day as part of the Hajj. It includes Hajra's run, stoning the Shaitaan, slaughtering an animal in honour of the sacrifice that Ibrahim made and going up to Mount Arafat from which the Prophet made his last sermon.

The Sacrifice

One night, Ibrahim had a dream. The dream shook him completely. He was asked by Allah to sacrifice somebody closest to his heart. His son Ismail was the closest to him. So, Ibrahim decided to sacrifice him in the path of Allah, even though he loved him a lot. Initially, he thought that Shaitaan was up to his tricks and that it wasn't a dream. Then he had the same vision the next night and he concluded it was a dream from Allah. So he took his son to Mount Arafat and took along a rope and a knife. The sacrifice was to be made there. Along the way, at Mina, they encountered Shaitaan who tried to talk Ibrahim out of it. He did not listen. Ibrahim headed to Mount Arafat with little Ismail. There he told him about his dream.

Ismail said if it was from Allah, it had to be done. He told his father to tie up his hands and feet first. Then tie a piece of cloth around his own eyes so as a father, Ibrahim's pain would be reduced. He advised his father to sharpen the knife for the sacrifice. Ibrahim did as told. He tied a cloth around his own eyes, lay his son down and moved his knife around the throat. When he opened his eyes, he was surprised. He had passed the knife over his son's throat but it was a ram that had been sacrificed. Ismail sat by his side. His son was exchanged for a ram by Allah. Ibrahim was worried. Then came a voice to assure him that he had done what was asked of him. His sacrifice is recounted, and performed again to this day on Eid-ul-Adha. Popularly but erroneously called Bakrid, this festival is not about sacrificing a goat (bakri) but recalling the sacrifice of Ibrahim.

Praying Together

The Hajj completes the epoch of the prayer cycle in the life of a Muslim. It begins with the local mosque in a colony where people are expected to pray five times a day. It goes up a notch on Friday when the community is expected to head to the biggest mosque in the city, usually the Jama Masjid. Incidentally, the word 'jama' itself stands for a collection or congregation. It goes up a step with Eid when one has to gather at the local Eidgah, at a large, open ground, the largest prayer place in the city. It culminates in the gathering of the community from across the world at Hajj. So from your local street, to people from different colonies to everybody in the city, and everybody from every nook and corner of the world, the prayer cycle is completed.

Everyday Dos

Prophet Muhammad gave a comprehensive list of dos and dont's to help his followers. For instance, he said that one should eat with the right hand and use the left hand at the toilet. Similarly, he said, one should enter the mosque with the right foot and leave with the left. The rules are reversed for attending our nature calls.

When we begin to eat, we have to begin with the name of Allah, 'Bismillah.' So important was saying 'Bismillah' for him that he said, if one forgets at the beginning, one can say whenever one remembers during the meal. Thus, if life has a little discipline and gratefulness and is filled with prayer, togetherness and peace, it can be a wonderful journey!

The Story of Karbala

We all know know of the legend of Daud , but only some people know that there was a battle in which seventy-two people won against thirty-thousand. It involved Hussein, the grandson of the Prophet. He rode out with his army and family towards Kufa in Iraq where Yazid's oppression knew no limits. The expedition though was intercepted and they moved towards Karbala. There was no relief here for Hussain and his companions. In the scorching desert, they were denied access to water for three days. Then Yazid issued orders to kill Hussain and his followers. They killed the men, but left the women and children, whom they took with them as prisoners.

Incidentally, the famed battle of Karbala took place on the tenth day of the Islamic month of Moharram, the first month of the Islamic calendar. In the battle, Hussain was beheaded by Shimr Ibn Thil-Jawshan; his martyrdom to this day evokes feelings of an unmitigated tragedy. Hussain became a symbol of the struggle of right against wrong.

Drink Water the Right Way

Islam provides a way of drinking water too! One should not drink water while standing as it affects the knees. One should sit facing the Kaaba and take water in three slow sips and conclude it with a prayer to Allah. After all, life is but a prayer in Islam.

All the Good Things

Often when we do not get a dish of our choice or do not get the clothes we would like to wear on that day, it irritates us and we get angry. The Prophet was not in favour of any such action. He wanted each one to be grateful for all the good things, big or small. Prophet Muhammad said, 'Whoever amongst you wakes up in the morning and is safe in his home, in good health and has enough provision for the day, it is as if he has all the good things in the world.'

ISBN: 978-93-84225-31-5

ISBN: 978-81-87107-53-8

ISBN: 978-81-87107-55-2

ISBN: 978-81-87107-52-1

ISBN: 978-93-80069-35-7

ISBN: 978-93-80070-84-1

ISBN: 978-93-80070-83-4

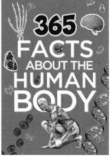
ISBN: 978-93-84625-93-1

ISBN: 978-93-83202-81-2

ISBN: 978-93-80070-79-7

ISBN: 978-93-84625-92-4

ISBN: 978-93-85031-29-8

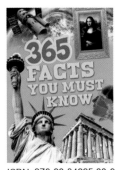
ISBN: 978-93-84225-33-9

ISBN: 978-93-84225-32-2

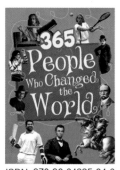
ISBN: 978-93-84225-34-6

ISBN: 978-81-87107-56-9

ISBN: 978-93-81607-49-7

ISBN: 978-81-87107-58-3

ISBN: 978-81-87107-57-6

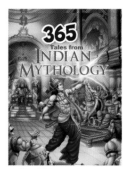
ISBN: 978-81-87107-46-0